CHICAGO SOCIALISM

*To Matt & Marcia,
with great gratitude and in
appreciation for the many years of friendship,
love and support!*

CHICAGO SOCIALISM

THE PEOPLE'S HISTORY

Joseph Anthony Rulli

27 August 2019

THE
History
PRESS

Published by The History Press
Charleston, SC
www.historypress.net

Front cover, top: Chicago Teachers Union demonstration, 1930s. *Courtesy of the Chicago History Museum*; *bottom*: A girl making a speech in downtown Chicago. *Courtesy of the Chicago History Museum* (CHM: i003200).

Back cover, left: May 1, 2014, at the Haymarket Memorial. *Courtesy of the author*; *right*: The Statue of Industry that originally stood above the entrance to the 1885 Board of Trade building. *Courtesy of Nathanael Filbert and Brad Seifert*.

First published 2019

Manufactured in the United States

ISBN 9781467141260

Library of Congress Control Number: 2019939741

Notice: The information in this book is true and complete to the best of our knowledge. It is offered without guarantee on the part of the author or The History Press. The author and The History Press disclaim all liability in connection with the use of this book.

[The Ghost said,] *"If he be like to die, he had better do it, and decrease the surplus population."*
Scrooge hung his head to hear his own words quoted by the spirit, and was overcome with penitence and grief.
"Man," said the Ghost, *"if man you be in heart, not adamant, forbear that wicked cant until you have discovered What the surplus is, and Where it is. Will you decide what men shall live, what men shall die? It may be, that in the sight of Heaven, you are more worthless and less fit to live than millions like this poor man's child. Oh God! To hear the Insect on the leaf pronouncing on the too much life among his hungry brothers in the dust!"*
—Charles Dickens, A Christmas Carol, *Stave III (1843)*

[Behold] *a city for sale and doomed to destruction, if it should find a buyer.*
—Sallust (86–35 B.C.E.), The Jugurthine War, *Book 35*

DEDICATION

This book is dedicated to the memories of

Felix Salvatore Rulli (1931–2017)
and
Catherine Marie (Palmero) Rulli (1930–2018)

Children of immigrants, lifelong laborers in the workplace and loving parents and grandparents in our family.

It is also dedicated to all laborers throughout the centuries and millennia across the globe, nameless to history, who have struggled for a more equitable and just world; to all who have suffered at the hands of their fellow human beings for speaking out in defense of others and who have been relegated to the tombs of the unknowns, the desaparecidos, the disappeared ones; and to the refugee, the enslaved, the burned, the butchered as victims of totalitarianism, racial and economic exploitation, fear and rabid nationalism. It is their story, here in small, that is told: a voice to the voiceless, defying language barriers, that speaks for them and for those who still suffer today, wandering homeless on their own planet, and all, sadly, who still suffer this fate. And to all those who build bridges and tear down walls while there is still time to change the pattern.

CONTENTS

CONTENTS

LIST OF PHOTOGRAPHS

LIST OF PHOTOGRAPHS

ACKNOWLEDGEMENTS

A book such as this comes about through hard work, diligence and a near-obsessive desire to present something dear to the heart. However, it is not created by the writer out of nothing. Others, in decades prior, have set about in research, writing articles and making charts and graphs to which the author has access. Many more people, in the present, directly affect the writer's success.

Firstly, I give my heartfelt thanks again to my family; to Cathy, Bill, Michael and Samantha Kazmierczak; and to Terri Rulli, with whom I share the most-common story. By association and blood, I also owe great gratitude to my extended family and all the people of South Bend, Mishawaka and Elkhart, Indiana—immigrants and descendants of immigrants who hold more in common with those who still come, the refugees and caravans of today, than some may realize.

As a lifelong lover of history, bibliophile and second-career writer, I thank the teachers (especially my English, social studies and theater guides), as well as the staffs of St. John the Baptist Catholic School, the Alexis Coquillard Public School Library, St. Joseph's High School, Holy Cross College, the University of Notre Dame and St. Meinrad School of Theology.

To the staff and supporters of the Chicago History Museum, especially in the Research Center, who were very attentive to me in my sometimes twice-a-week visits into the directories, microfilms and maps: Ellen Keith, Leslie Martin, Michael Featherstone, Gretchen Neidhardt, Ariel Robinson and Noel Dwyer. Many thanks also to Angela Hoover and the Rights and Reproduction Department for their time, patience and good humor and to those who work with the photographic archive. To the staff of all the departments of the Newberry Library, among them Maggie Cusick, John Powell, Caleb Britton, Rosie Frehe and Patrick Reilly, I give an abundance of thanks for your professionalism, dedication and passion for the preservation and exhibition of the good, the bad and the ugly of the greatest city in the world.

To my friends near and far who have suffered my history (and histrionic) obsessions or babbling on with the details of this work during its birthing: your enthusiasm and curiosity, again, have been energizing and spurred me on to complete the project.

A large amount of my gratitude is to the city of Chicago and surrounding municipalities and all their connected services, particularly the Chicago Transit Authority and Metra lines. I have been a regular passenger of trains and buses since arriving here in the winter of 2006 and can say that using public transportation is second nature for me. The economic benefits, the ease of travel and my always-spicy fellow riders have allowed me to get to where I need to be in a timely (most of the time) and safe manner. This book would be a lot different, a lot less accurate and a lot duller had I not been able to go and check out sites firsthand whenever the whim struck. To the Chicago Police Department, for their daily sacrifices and risks taken for public safety and for the ongoing efforts of those working with communities to find constructive solutions to our problems.

To the Edgy Writers of the bimonthly workshops, my (almost) speechless gratitude for your honest input, critique and support in the fictional and nonfictional parts of my world. Your presence with me at our gatherings and at my individual readings and play performances heartens me constantly. And, by extension, my thanks go to the staffs at Zanzibar Café and Nookies in Edgewater, without whom our meetings would be drier and a bit more tasteless.

To my financial and techno-teams in the digital and corporeal realms: my photographer, Nathanael Filbert, and his assistant Brad Seifert; my web designer, MacDaniel Sullivan; and my financial guru, Mark Willis—all gratitude pours out to you for the selfless sharing of your gifts with me. Without your work, this book would be greatly impoverished.

To the staff at The History Press for their belief in and excitement for this project, most of whom I have not met in person. I give most heartfelt thanks to Ben Gibson, my commissioning editor, for his passion about the material and for the guidance he has provided me in this, our second endeavor; and to my copy editor, Sara Miller, for her eagle eyes, wit and thoughtfulness.

Once again, to my coworkers and management at Trader Joe's on Clybourn Avenue, my day-in, day-out companions in this life we're sharing—you make a potential drudgery a true joy. Also, thanks to the Trader Joe's Company, which has given me employment and financial security for over a decade, giving me the luxury of time to complete my second book while being employed by them.

A heartfelt thanks again to my comrades in the socialist, anarchist and communist camps: your passionate and peaceful presence in the city—from the Occupy events to the annual May Day and teachers' rallies, protests, marches and conferences—proves that liberty still has a voice, and it's not the one piped through the mainstream. To my comrade, fellow writer and friend Robert Kingett.

Lastly, and most passionately, I repeat my thanks to all those workers of our past upon whose shoulders we've been supported; to humanity's missionaries who gave their lives in service to the poorest, especially Jean Donovan (1953–1980) and Archbishop Oscar Romero (1917–1980); to the philosophers and organizers of a budding socialist movement across the globe in the nineteenth century; and to those who suffered under fascist repression in the twentieth century, most affectionately to Antonio Gramsci (1891–1937). Their blood, sweat and tears have reaped a harvest of a more just society than was known 150 years ago. Though we've not come as far as some had hoped, we have come further than many had dreamed because of them.

Liberty, equality, fraternity to all!

PREFACE

All Hail Chicago! I would that I could come; and more, I would that I could stay. The unselfish devotion to Labor Emancipation that I saw during my visit last year [from Boston] *remains as a pleasant vision….Remember me to the committee as one with them, and to all as in bonds with them, restless under chains, yet biding the time when we can be free in the possession of our own…. Thanks to Chicago for the work well done. Count me with you, though absent, to rescue the day from capitalistic control. Let Chicago's streets be filled.*[1]
—*George E. McNeill, letter to* The Socialist, *June 2, 1879*

This work is born of an admittedly left bend and a fascination for Chicago history. I've come to be a lover of history honestly; since I can remember, I've always read and enjoyed it, falling head over heels for *Johnny Tremain*. I was eleven years old when the United States turned two hundred in 1976, and collected all I could that was red, white and blue. I had the *Arrow Book of Presidents* (1972 and 1976 editions) to track the elections of those years.

By the time of the 1980 presidential election, the left tilt was in motion. I was a sophomore at St. Joe High School in South Bend and a nonvoting member of the Democratic Party. I fumed in speechless anger (okay, maybe not totally devoid of speech) when I found out that my parents had joined countless others of their generation and voted as part of a new monstrosity called "Reagan Democrats."

The odiousness of this phrase could be tolerated for the next twelve years (past the reigns of Ronald Reagan and George Bush I) only by my donning a red scarf in the winter to counter the Great Communicator's white one that flapped in the wind as I watched, on the nightly news, the chief executive boarding and deplaning Air Force One during his countless jaunts across the globe, spreading American propaganda far and wide—I have a flair for the dramatic…and the symbolic. I registered for the draft out of obedience—and, honestly, I needed the scholarship money for college that hung in front of me as the carrot to get me to put myself in a potential lineup for slaughter.

I campaigned for Walter Mondale in 1984 and heard him speak in Chicago just before he was crushed in the November election. My great "liberal" views were peeled away as William Jefferson Clinton dragged the executive office through the filth of his scandals and lies to reveal politicians' bipartisan pettiness and conniving as they climbed the rungs of power. Having very briefly given the Republican Party a listening ear, I realized that the one-party system that's in place—that of the capitalist party—needed to be abandoned. It is with that twenty-year-old conviction that this book has come about with the hope that this democratic republic, established two and a half centuries ago, can be salvaged by a realistic and honest reappraisal of what has developed.

My fascination with and love for Chicago are centered on its unique story as well as the constancy of those who have struggled to retell the history in a more complete light. Something happened early on that targeted the "City on the Lake" for prestige in the pantheon of big cities. The native peoples in the area named the swampy territory "checagou," ("onion-smelling") and it stuck—so did the odor, literally and metaphorically. The early French and English settlers, after dispensing with the Potawatomi and Miami, began the trade and building that would lead to Chicago's rise from the murky water. Canals and railroads were built, and more immigrants poured in (there were no quotas or walls back then), along with money. Soon, the vision dawned of bigger everything—buildings, businesses and graft.

Destroying angels have decimated many cities, from Rome, London and San Francisco to Tokyo and Berlin. However, few leaders have harnessed energy from all quarters of its population and around the world as Chicago did after the 1871 fire. Within a few years, an urban center remade itself, and over the subsequent decades, the "Second City" that rose from ash bullied its neighbors with chutzpa and bravado, raising its stature on the world stage, reversing the flow of a river, raising the entire level of the city, renumbering its address system and, even today, keeping a political machine well-oiled and at the service of its patrons.

I look to a blended representative democracy, devoid (as much as is possible) of special-interest dictation of local and national policy, stripped of money-based powerbrokers and cleansed of the semblance of backroom and back-alley dealings. Human beings have a limited time in this world, and it should extend to the political life as well, with universal term limits for elected and appointed officials. If we are in possession of a real republic founded on democratic principles, then a new approach to universal enfranchisement is necessary.

A word is necessary on historical perspective and its relation to the present political and cultural debating. The signers of the Declaration of Independence in 1776 made a choice, for the sake of a unified front against the British, to table the issue of slavery. But one may ask, what would have happened if the young republic, formed in the aftermath of revolution, picked up the revolutionary idea of universal emancipation in the next generation? What if the concerns of the individual southern plantation owner (concerned about economic survival and fending off an encroaching federal government) were gradually addressed? What if a "weaning off" of slave labor had been implemented by the 1820s? What if the slaves had been granted emancipation and recognition of their full humanity with employment opportunities underwritten by federal and state governments? (If Civil War expenditures are taken into account, there would have been ample funding had there been no war between the states.) Had something like this been introduced around the time of Abraham Lincoln's birth (1809), perhaps by the time he was an adult, a more robust southern economy with a fully enfranchised and self-sufficient African American population would have resulted.

We won't ever know what might have been, but we do know the blood, carnage and lynchings that did happen by not following that path.

Rational debate rooted in basic respect for one another is key to finding viable solutions to all issues we face. When one side demonizes the other, compromise becomes very difficult—why would one find a middle ground with absolute evil? The days of contentious invective and vitriol have got to be left in the past so that we can, in the present, find satisfactory answers and hand over a better society to those who will follow us.

The structure of this work follows a loose chronology, looking back and then forward again in a more or less thematic pattern. Periods of time are scanned for their highlights with regard to socialism in elections, labor issues, education, racial and ethnic relations, issues regarding women, journalism and the world stage. This book is meant to be a brief perusal of Chicago history with a starting point of just after the Civil War. This history is told in relation to the Socialist Party itself, the homegrown or adopted members of the party and the issues they raised and changes they pioneered. It is for other works to dive more deeply into each specific area covered in these pages.

Chapter I

AN INTRODUCTION: A WOMAN IN RED WHO READ...AND WROTE IN THE CITY ON THE MAKE

While the Democratic Party stands for the welfare of the middle class [and the Republican Party stands for the welfare of the upper class] *under the present system...the Socialist Party stands for the welfare of all the people through its advocacy of the abolition of our present insane system of production and distribution of the necessities of life.*[2]
—Josephine Conger-Kaneko (Socialist candidate for alderman, Sixth Ward, 1914)

She had a socialistic journal in Chicago—known under the names the *Socialist Woman*, the *Progressive Woman* and the *Coming Nation*—with a print run from 1907 until the outbreak of the First World War in 1914. She received support from national and international figures such as fellow Socialists Eugene Debs and Emma Goldman as well as British author George Bernard Shaw. She worked for women's suffrage and saw its attainment in Illinois in 1913—seven years before the Nineteenth Amendment made voting rights for women federal law.

Josephine Conger-Kaneko participated in and chronicled the political life of the Socialist Party in Chicago after the "revolutionary generation," those who had been witness to and lived under the reaction against the Haymarket Riot of 1886. Her generation contained a more sedate socialistic element that returned to the polls and the soapboxes under the example of Debs and Mother Jones. No less committed, no less principled and no less intelligent than the previous generation, she and her peers sought to change American society from the ground up. Chicago was to

A girl making a speech in downtown Chicago. *Courtesy of the Chicago History Museum* (CHM: i003200).

be the foundation; floating on a swamp, as it was, it would be the big shoulders upon which the workers could stand taller and stronger to usher in the social revolution of the world.

Chicago, the "City on the Make," on the take, take-what-you-can, make sure you don't get caught. It's a city that has reeked of dead carcasses from stockyards and, to this day, reels from a stench out of its city hall. It is a city that has risen to amazing heights from swamp to ash and was resurrected in steel and concrete while, at the same time, sinking to depths of depravity and greed, good-old-boyism and nepotism of the Caligula/Nero breed.

The story of Chicago socialism is, like the story of the city itself, unique. The men and women who embraced the philosophy of a better world through social and political change saw the urban battlefield as essential to attaining the goal and Chicago as the springboard. Though other cities had active socialist parties, radical reform elements and even violent clashes that could have sparked a revolution, Chicago was seen as the most vibrant.

When violence broke out across the country in the summer of 1877 during the nationwide railroad strike, Chicago bore witness to twenty out of the one hundred deaths. While states' militias were called up to quell the rioting, many of the soldiers refused to take up arms against the workers. This was not the case in Chicago: police, Illinois national guardsmen and federal troops battled civilians over several days, including during the two-day "Battle of the Viaduct" and subsequent brutal attack on Vorwärts Turner Hall, located at Halsted and Twelfth Streets, where a furniture workers' meeting was taking place. The authorities had stormed the building after chasing men from the nearby battleground and began to pummel workers at random in the classic dystopian tactic of setting the haystack on fire to find the needle. This happened in Chicago.

These incidents served to embolden the socialist cause into the next decade with tragic effects in continual violence, which should have served as warning signs that social conditions in the Second City were close to explosive and that it might not simply be buildings that would get leveled.

In all of this, there comes a time for change, and not of the political stripe of simply pulling off one nameplate from an office door and replacing it with a different one—an "R" for a "D," or vice versa. The history of Chicago too often tells the tales of the well-known, the well-to-do, the well-off—those who have gained from the perpetuation of the status quo. Over the past two centuries, tens of thousands have been left behind, trampled underfoot, left out in the cold and outside of the story of the city.

The goal of this book is twofold: first, to present as clear a "popular" history (literally, from the perspective of the populi—the people) of socialism in Chicago as is possible, and second, to promote a platform for political discourse that can be seen as part of the solution to the oligarchic (rule by a few elites) intransigence of the political system in this city as well as this nation since the end of the Second World War.

It is reasonable to suppose that a clear-cut choice between representative democracy solely fueled by either capitalism or socialism is untenable. History has shown what happens when human beings seek to establish a society comprised only of those who can "pull themselves up by their own bootstraps," on the one hand, or in building a worker's paradise, on the other. We don't have a good track record here, as countless men, women and children in coal mines and garment mills have attested along with millions more who have been displaced or eliminated in pogroms, work camps, killing fields and state cooperatives.

The solution must consider the reality of many people occupying space on the same orbiting rock with few options at this time except to live with each other as harmoniously as possible. Even leaving open the possibility of colonizing other planets floating along with us in this galaxy or farther off, we still carry in us that seed of humanity, in all its brilliance and debauchery, that no one will leave behind even if jettisoned light years away to another planet. Each of the several billion people currently on this planet has an equal right to life, liberty and the pursuit of happiness here and now, no matter their shape, age, color, political persuasion, religious belief or unbelief, clothing preference, gender preference or any other category we can conceive of to make distinctions to flavor our lives.

Step one is understanding, so let's begin by stating the basic Merriam-Webster definitions of some key concepts:

CAPITALISM is an economic system characterized by private corporate ownership of saleable (capital) goods, by investments that are determined by private decisions and by prices, production and the distribution of goods that are determined mainly by competition in a free market.

SOCIALISM is an umbrella term describing a variety of economic systems advocating collective (social) or government ownership and administration of the means of production and distribution of goods.

COMMUNISM refers both to a system in which goods are owned in common (therefore, no private property) and available to all according to need, as well as referring to the final stage of society in Marxist theory whereby the state disappears and goods are distributed equitably according to need.

Step two is accepting the fact that none of these definitions contains the totality of the concepts themselves—there are exceptions, variances and multiple opinions related to these three major systems; it's a lot like trying to define Judaism, Christianity, Islam, Hinduism or Buddhism in two or three sentences. I merely use standard definitions of these economic theories to provide a framework for this brief history with an eye to proposing a more workable political system "in order to form a more perfect union." Okay, maybe the actual reach of this book is not so grandiose, but I am still committed to offering a guide to begin the escape from the mean-spirited, invective-filled swamp in which we find ourselves in Chicago and the United States in the first quarter of the twenty-first century.

Socialism in Chicago can be a contradictory tale depending on who's telling it. The goal of this book is not to split the difference or to choose a side. This work strives to see the historical realities in as objective a view as possible, albeit imperfectly and skewed, looking at socialist principles (and capitalism's fears of them) rooted in the mother of proletariat uprisings, the French Revolution of 1789. This is done with a focus on the Windy City, protecting the reader, of course, from the gusts of political hot air that have now been blowing across three centuries.

As the nineteenth century dawned in the blood soaking of the post–French Revolution "Reign of Terror," detractors have shown just what happens when the people get to power, as if monarchies and capitalistic democracies have been somehow guided by a benevolence from above bestowing goodness and kindness and mercy to all. Socialism, in the past two centuries, was born in despair. The ruling class, whether wearing a crown or a top hat, sat on the serf, the farmer and the wage laborer like a lid on boiling water—and the lid had burst off on several occasions since the close of the eighteenth century, and more so since the beginning of recorded history.

This book seeks to balance the accounting in the historical record of "giving credit where credit is due." It's in this vein that the story is traced in Chicago but from a more face-to-face view of the average citizen and local politician. It is true that what was sparked in Paris in 1789 grew to wildfire status in 1877 in the United States as a railroad strike spread during a two-week war of capital against labor with over one hundred people dead. The violent response to economic pressure exploded in the Haymarket Riot on Chicago's west side in 1886. The pattern would repeat (more and less violently) in the 1894 Pullman Strike; the 1919 race riots; the garment-district strikes, steel strikes, red scares and other upheavals of the 1960s; the labor issues of the latter part of the twentieth century and beginning of the

Harper's Weekly, chronicling the 1877 Battle of the Viaduct and attack on Vorwärts Turner Hall. *Courtesy of the Chicago History Museum* (CHM: i019665_pm).

Present-day Halsted and Sixteenth Streets, the site of the 1877 Battle of the Viaduct. *Courtesy of Nathanael Filbert.*

twenty-first; and the protests against police use of excessive force and silence in the face of sexual abuse (in dressing rooms and boardrooms and churches) into the second decade of this century.

These major events are worthy of a detailed chronicling in their own right but are beyond the scope of this work. This book studies life-changing events as they relate to the citizens of Chicago, the people—in all the charm of Midwesterners (blood-born and adopted), in all the strength of raising up a city from ash, in all the varied flavors of race and ethnicity, in all the shadiness of manipulators of elections, in all the arrogance of those who defy the rule of law (sometimes by the purported upholders of that same law), in all the brazenness of the builders of towering masses that scrape the sky—living together on top of *checagou*, the onion-smelling swamp that has a hidden side, and it is this lesser-known story that will be told here.

The late nineteenth and early twentieth centuries saw the construction of systematic platforms, methodologies, schools of thought and programs of action from the left side of the political spectrum. In Chicago, socialist leadership struggled at the ballot box for recognition, even as it wrestled with established power brokers to keep meddling hands from stuffing their pockets year-round or stifling the voices of the people on Election Day. This newborn leadership found itself performing a balancing act between a staid group willing to make changes vote-by-vote and a militant wing, born of the European upheavals of the 1848 revolutionary period, that was more likely to throw a bomb rather than their hat into the ring.

These two "left sides" would merge as machine corruption in Chicago alienated voters and candidates of the Socialist Party. By 1883, all but the most idealistic had abandoned the hope of change through the electoral process. The spring of 1886 saw the first nationwide strike for an eight-hour workday, the first nationwide recognition of May 1 as a worker holiday and the first civilian bombing in the country. The Haymarket Riot, interpreted in vastly different ways even to this day, has been a major factor in U.S. attitudes on labor issues, socialism and government power.

The Russian Revolution of 1917 provides the hallmark for most politically-minded people—"left" or "right"—in terms of the most influential event (aside from war) that shaped the twentieth century. A new type of war, a "cold" one, was invented, and waging this eight-decade struggle carried

Demonstration in Chicago, late 1960s. *Courtesy of the Chicago History Museum* (CHM: i019625_pm).

the belligerents into old-fashioned "hot" wars in eastern Europe, Korea, southeast Asia, Afghanistan (with the Russian Bear rampaging through that area before Uncle Sam did) and Central and South America. Chicago was not immune to the strife, as lists were drawn up and suspected "reds" were watched and sometimes rounded up, blacklisted and/or targeted for more nefarious ends as Mayor Richard J. Daley (the first Mayor Daley) gave venomous teeth to the Chicago Police Department's Red Squad.

A brand of socialism rising in the first half of the twenty-first century has sought to address the apparent impotence of socialist parties of the past and present. The now-incapacitated International Socialist Organization (ISO) had worked to build a movement "from below," and it has presently fallen to other organizations to pick up the banner. Using the momentum of popular protests, enshrined as *the* way to go in the United States since the Civil Rights and anti–Vietnam War Movements, more grassroots organizing has borne fruit in sustained levels of popular commitment in all parts of the country. In Chicago, this has been realized in antiviolence, anti-abuse, anti–police brutality, pro–gun control, pro-teacher, pro-immigrant and pro-right-to-marry rallies. The Occupy movements in Chicago and across the country in 2011 and 2012 brought popular protest to the forefront of the world stage again, as did the yellow vests of France moving across Europe.

Chapter 2

THE CRY OF A PEOPLE: CHICAGO'S STORY WAS NOT BORN IN A VACUUM

We are exceedingly impoverished. All supplies for us...have been allowed to be exhausted. Let our Lord make for us a means of keeping us alive![3]

This plea could have been heard in the nineteenth century, echoing from a boy scraping animal sludge from a Chicago slaughterhouse floor, or from a woman in present-day east Africa waiting in line for a bowl of rice. It actually comes from a man, speaking on behalf of many, who was working on a tomb in the Valley of the Queens under Ramesses III over three thousand years ago and reached gargantuan proportions as the voice of the first recorded labor strike on the planet around 1182 B.C.E.

Jettisoning ahead of the above and up the Mediterranean Sea to the Italian Peninsula in 494 B.C.E., the plebeians of Rome literally walked out of the city in protest against the patrician class's refusal to grant concessions to the common people (well, at least to the common man) for more of a say in the senate. After the shutdown of most day-to-day activities, the elites realized just how little control they held and granted some of the demands. Most importantly, they established the office of Tribune of the People, which became—for a couple centuries, anyway—the voice of the plebeians in the senate. The walkout happened again in the third century B.C.E. as a reminder to those who had forgotten that balance is key to more than just a gladiator thrusting a lance at a lion.

In a less than victorious example of the laboring class's struggle, we have the serf of the Middle Ages who lived in feudal servitude. Sadly, this practice

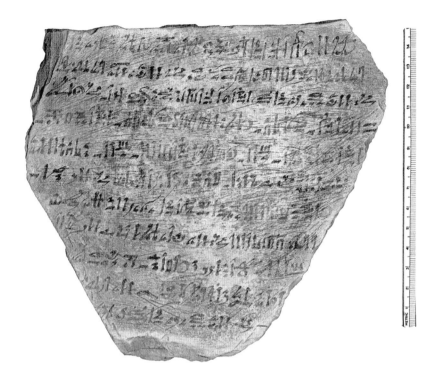

Letter of complaint from a tomb-builder to the pharaoh Ramesses III. *Courtesy of the Oriental Institute of the University of Chicago.*

is rearing its head today as lending institutions and universities hold an entire generation under the chattel of student debt, keeping the twenty-first-century serf under the control of the "lords of the manor," Sallie Mae and Freddie Mac, with the blessings and legal legitimacy of the lawyer/banker gods in the U.S. House of Representatives and Senate.

The cry of a people is more than simply a whimper during bad times. It is the evoking of an inner voice that screams for freedom. The liberation always comes, either in life or by death, and it will always serve as a harbinger of change, no matter how slow or miniscule, in the social order. It has consistently been an unheeded warning to those who wield power over people who see their fate as to merely submit. In the colonial era of the late sixteenth century and well into the twentieth, the slave trade and its residual scars represent capitalism's most tragic side. The complete denial of humanity of Africans and native residents of North and South America became economic doctrine to fuel the pillaging of Africa and the

Western Hemisphere for the enrichment of Europe, and, by extension, North American merchants, bankers and Founding Fathers. With native culture relegated to reservations, parades and local history museums, the ruling class has succeeded in the extermination of an entire people's past on the American continents. Descendants of the African slave trade still reel in response to a culture's slow admission of guilt for three centuries of abduction and abuse—an underlying cause of this nation's shameful legacy of poverty, crime and early death in African American communities.

After a volcano has violently erupted, people in the area around the crater are leery of future explosions. Chicago settled into this uneasiness after the Civil War and the Great Railroad Strike of 1877, as well as in the months following the 1886 bombing and the executions of four of the eight people convicted in the Haymarket Riot. Little changed in terms of attitudes. Wages remained low, education of children was stunted due to their need to provide income for the family rather than attend school and the economy rose and

Lithograph of Christopher Columbus in a pose demonstrative of the colonial attitude of superiority in the Age of Exploration. *Courtesy of the Chicago History Museum.*

fell with little regard for the human toll. Industrialists, speculators and other power brokers continued on their diligent path to more wealth, riding on the backs of the working class—and on government handouts.

The legend of the "self-made man" has got to be unmasked. A newborn Chicago (and those who made their first bags of money) received land grants, through the State of Illinois, from the federal government. The "Booster Generation," those who received this land as early as 1840, began the construction of the canal system that would eventually connect the Mississippi River to trade in the Great Lakes, with Chicago as the major urban link.[4] At the same time, land was given to these early entrepreneurs to extend the railroad system that, in a few decades, would connect the East and West Coasts, uniting the country, improving communication and trade and amassing fortunes for those who controlled these steel and timber arteries—but not for those who built them. At every turn of track, workers built the rail lines, and into the next century, they continually had to fight for just wages and improved working conditions.

On the eve of civil war, in 1860, the "Manufacturing Generation" came to the fore. These were the industrialists who came to Chicago and made the first clink of coin by producing household goods, farm equipment and food—this group included Marshall Field, Cyrus McCormick and Phillip Armour, among many others.[5] When war came the following year, they were poised to receive contracts from the Grand Army of the Republic to provide the necessities that would be required for years of carnage and destruction. Government money, again, served as the springboard for the creation of massive wealth that survives to this day in family fortunes and foundation works.

Rather than a tirade against money or the entrepreneurial spirit, this is a reminder of the historical reality showing that no one makes money ex nihilo (out of nothing). It's true that wealth is accumulated by hard work and diligence, but it is also gotten on agreement with laborers whose only avenue to making a living might be working for someone who has received this favored opportunity. One can give props to a deity who can create everything out of nothing with a read of the book of Genesis, but not to a group of speculators, born with the right skin pigmentation and genitalia, who happened to be in the right place at the right time and possessed an individualism that has historically tended to disregard most of the rest of their fellow citizens.

The balancing of the account books in relation to those who have benefitted from the handouts of federal, state and local governments is

A servant in the Leander McCormick household, circa 1888. *Courtesy of the Chicago History Museum* (CHM: i030808).

essential to understanding socialism in Chicago and throughout the United States. If a segment of the citizenry is going to be chastised for receiving public money, the record needs to be opened in toto: "big business" was allowed to grow large because of government tax breaks, land grants and insider information leading to large gains amassed due to speculation of the stock market—information not available to the average citizen. Much of this money has come in the form of corporate handouts, which, in reality, offer money for no work.

If fiscal conservatives insist on a welfare program of money for work for the individual, which makes sense, then there must be a comparable expectation and mandate for businesses. If corporations receive a tax break—with budgetary ramifications for the city, state and/or nation—they ought to be held accountable in terms of contributing to the community to which they owe some of their abundance. This is the motive behind granting tax-free status to religious organizations; the idea is that these groups remove some of the burden from government agencies in areas such as charitable work, hospital administration and education.

What has been accomplished with the fuel that capital provides, the individual incentive to succeed and the boldness to realize what had once only been a dream is indisputable. Human beings have cured innumerable diseases, provided for the advancement of culture and reached into the galaxy beyond our "big blue marble." This is even more reason to expect that the promotion of the good of all would be a constant in the forefront of our collective mind. An end to hunger and malnutrition through the teaching of basic farming methods, universal education as a right, arbitration of conflicts through rational discussion, clean air and soil and water conservation, the limitation of the collective carbon footprint through a hallowing of the planet (the only thing we completely hold in common)—these are the attainable things for which we can strive. If we have already taken the scientific, economic and cultural journey, the other necessities of life and peaceful coexistence are more likely to come.

Chapter 3

FROM HOPE TO HAYMARKET: ELECTIONS, LABOR, GOD AND REVOLUTION IN THE NINETEENTH CENTURY

[It is resolved on behalf of the Trade and Labor Council of Chicago and vicinity to appoint] *a special committee to examine into the condition of the working classes…to gather information in order to enact laws to ameliorate the condition of workers in Illinois.*[6]
—*Christian Meier (Socialist, Sixth District, Illinois House of Representatives), February 2, 1879*

In early 1879, following the midterm elections of the previous fall, Socialist candidates scored major victories by winning election to municipal and state offices in Chicago and Illinois. It had been less than eighteen months since the bloody national railroad strike, the "Great Upheaval," of 1877. The brutal repression of the strike by police, state militias and federal troops from West Virginia to the West Coast caused the bubbling up of resentments against Democrats and Republicans, particularly in large cities.

To further stretch tolerance and patience to their breaking points, the result of the 1876 presidential election had been contentious, to say the least. For the first time (but not the last), the candidate who won the popular vote, Democrat Samuel Tilden, lost the electoral vote to Republican Rutherford Hayes. In fact, for a time, Tilden had tallied 184 electoral votes to Hayes's 165, with 20 votes unresolved (representing the electoral count in Florida, Louisiana, South Carolina and Oregon). After much finagling, pomposity, wheeling and dealing, Hayes was declared the winner, and the Democrat-controlled southern states (in exchange for their support of Hayes) were promised an end to Reconstruction-era occupation by federal troops; newly enfranchised (and soon-to-be disenfranchised) African Americans in Dixie would see ol' Jim Crow grow to horrific power over the next hundred years.

The Socialists offered an alternative. The Workingmen's Party of Illinois, the voice of Chicago's New Left, was established in 1874, and two years later, during the centennial of the nation, it merged with the Workingmen's Party of America with the goal of nationalizing the railroads and all telegraph lines.[7] By 1878, the party was advocating for voting rights for women, an abolition of child labor and an eight-hour cap on the workday as planks in the official party platform.[8] The Socialist Party, which did not run its first candidate for mayor until two years later, watched the 1877 municipal elections with relish as Chicago's relatively new political machine churned and the game-players fed off of each other. Incumbent mayor Monroe Heath defeated Democratic contender Perry Smith in what would be one of the city's earliest displays of political cynicism; as the *Chicago Daily News* stated, "In order to elect Heath every honest man must go to the polls and vote. The thugs will be sure to *vote early and often* [emphasis by the author] for Smith."[9]

The Socialists saw their strength grow in the Fifth, Sixth, Seventh, Fourteenth, Fifteenth and Sixteenth Wards, with three wards each bringing in at least five hundred votes for the new party and the remaining three tallying over one thousand each. The Fourteenth Ward brought in the first Socialist victory as Frank Stauber won a seat on the city council.[10] Stauber would win reelection into the early 1880s. After two years in office, he was praised by *The Socialist* for his support of the "amelioration of the working classes" with the establishment of public baths, free libraries, adequate sewage systems in the poorer neighborhoods, oil lighting of streets and, most importantly (according to the paper), "the unearthing of the *rebate steal* [emphasis in original] by which over $300,000 [about $7.6 million today] was returned to the tax-payers."[11] Apparently, for over a decade, the practice of the city's comptroller, unnamed by the paper, had been to tap into the interest of this mysterious sum of money, pocketing it and doling it out to friends as a quiet bonus for their selfless civil service.

Of course, the reigning party (Republicans controlled things in those days) handily won the 1877 mayoral race by over twelve thousand votes, and the stage (or, more apropos, the backroom) was set for more electoral shenanigans that would continue into the next decade, alienating a large portion of Chicagoans and tickling the trigger fingers of anarchists waiting for an opportunity to strike. This era marks tremendous growth in the city fathers' rule by divine right of patronage, intimidation, thuggery and blatant criminality. It also marks the beginning of the sad story of an entire urban population giving themselves over to the cronyism that has made this city infamous. Across the board in the city, with only a few notable exceptions, these public officers initiated (and taxpayers sponsored) the buffet dinner of privilege, wealth and lifetime careers for themselves and their progeny—keep in mind the number of father-son, father-daughter, husband-wife, father-in-law-son-in-law successions that have occurred in Chicago and in Illinois. It's not a coincidence that several officeholders have had and still have a shared last name—and they continue to be reelected.

Springfield saw red (the real red, not the nickname applied by the U.S. media to the Republican Party) for the first time after the 1878 election brought four Socialists to the state capital—one senator (Sylvester Artley) and three representatives (Leonard Melbeck, Charles Ehrhardt and Christian Meier).[12] The first real opportunity for Socialist control of Chicago came in the spring of 1879, during the biennial municipal elections. Mayoral candidate Ernest Schmidt harnessed the momentum of the fall election victories and earned 11,829 votes—20 percent of the total. It was not enough to win against Carter Harrison the first, but it was enough to knock some ashes off cigars in city hall as the Workingmen's Party's (referred to in various circles simply as the Socialist Party) first splash into the political pool. The bravado carried the day and was expressed in *The Socialist*, Chicago's main sounding board of the party:

> These [electoral] tables ought to be conclusive proof that Socialism is taking deep root with the working people of this city, and our majority would have been greatly increased had not many manufacturers shown an indisposition to permit their employees to leave their shops for any length of time [in order to vote].[13]

Keep in mind that the workday for most laborers began around 6:00 a.m. and could extend past the twelve-hour mark. There were no extended hours at the polls, nor was there early voting. Low voter turnouts usually benefit whichever party is occupying the throne at any particular time; Democrats and Republicans in the city and nation have tended to take turns planting their seats behind the desk.

During the spring of 1879, in the city council, incumbent aldermen were rattled, even if they shifted only slightly in their chamber seats, as the "Red Wave" sent ripples across the city with the ever-strong Fifth, Sixth,

Lumber workers in Chicago, 1871. *Courtesy of the Chicago History Museum.*

Seventh, Fourteenth, Fifteenth and Sixteenth Wards each surpassing the one-thousand-vote mark for Socialist candidates and the party scoring three council seats, with J.J. Altpeter in the Sixth, R. Lorenz in the Fourteenth and Christian Meier in the Sixteenth Wards, in addition to Frank Stauber winning reelection in the Fourteenth Ward. (The city council was comprised of two aldermen per ward until 1923.) The Socialist candidate in the more modest Eighth Ward won over five hundred votes.[14]

Granted, these would not turn out to be lasting threats to the established order, but the election of 1879 marked the first time in Chicago's history that a viable third party—advocating radical change for the city, state and society in general—had scored such impressive tallies. It would also be the last time Socialist polling results would be so strong in the city until the municipal elections in the spring of 2019. Even as Eugene Debs surpassed 900,000 votes (6 percent of the popular vote) in the 1912 presidential election, vote counts for his fellow Socialists in Chicago's mayoral elections in 1911 and 1915 hovered under 25,000—and this without the legislative victories in City Hall or Springfield that socialists had gained the generation before. A fractured left, splintered by Democrat/Republican legislation during World War I, ran three candidates for mayor in 1919, after the war. Combined, the votes (nearly 82,000) for these three candidates were dwarfed by incumbent Mayor William Hale Thompson's almost 260,000 votes,[15] but had those combined votes been for one solidly-backed candidate, the postwar economic, labor and racial tensions in Chicago might have provided a springboard for victory in the next decade. Speculative history can be useful in that it can guide present-day reflection and action.

In 1879, accusations of electoral chicanery abounded, with more than just the Socialists complaining. The *Chicago Daily News* records Republican challengers in one precinct of the notoriously crooked First Ward protesting thirty Democratic votes cast by only six voters (that's five votes per voter, by the way). It was also recorded that in the First Ward, "from thirty to forty negroes [sic] attempted but failed to swear in their votes."[16] Of course, the cries from the capitalistic parties got little sympathy from the left's press. *The Socialist* editorials after the election agreed with the protests from the Republicans but held them responsible for part of the criminality in the process. "It [the accusations of the Republicans against the Democrats] is but a corroboration of our former statement of the capitalistic parties having combined to defeat the workingman at all hazards."[17]

In a letter to the editor of *The Socialist*, Frank Stauber noted that he had interviewed streetcar workers of the West Division Street Railway Company on Milwaukee Avenue who claimed to have been threatened with dismissal by their foremen had they not voted for the Republican ticket. They were escorted to the polling places by company men to verify that their votes had been cast—and cast for very specific candidates.[18]

It was only after citizens could no longer ignore the stench and putrid taste of electoral fraud that mechanisms were put in place to curb (but, of course, not eradicate) the excesses of the political machine that kept those in power powerful and those who were not (relatively) powerless. Reform started in the election process as early as 1885 with the establishment of the Chicago Board of Election Commissioners as overseers of practice and the placing of one judge with the power to appoint election officials. Since the beginning (of Chicago, anyway), the members of the county board had exerted control over election proceedings. All seems well and good on paper, but when the board is controlled by, for example, in the words of the 1915 Chicago Board of Election Commissioners reviewers, "the Van Pelt-McDonald 'gang' [early Chicago's movers/shakers of the day]," problems abound.[19]

The commission's task was to address the issues of repetitious voting, withholding of ballots by judges at precincts, outright stealing of ballots from the boxes, changing of the locations of polling places at will, hiring henchmen to intimidate voters at the polling places, altering ballots and returns, bribery and other practices that still, to this day, can raise questions surrounding the legitimacy of Chicago elections.[20]

In 1879, with votes cast, challenges made and offices contested, the city settled into an uneasy working peace. The plan was to begin to set things right in the workplace according to Socialist principles, or so the left hoped. Less than a month after the elections in Chicago, and with only four months elapsed since the November midterm elections, Socialists led an eight-member delegation from the Illinois House of Representatives on an inspection tour of "different portions of the city where workers reside [to look into] the general conditions and requirements of the wage workers."[21]

On March 1, 1879, in Parlor O of the Palmer House Hotel, this delegation met with representatives of the trade and labor unions of the city. Among the union reps and members of the Socialistic Labor Party were Thomas J. Morgan, local politician and native-born Englishman, who consistently ran for municipal offices into the next century and put into the legislative record that the work of the committee "was necessary to protect their [workers'] rights and interests, and secure to them the just rewards of their labor."[22] Also in attendance was Texas native and Confederate army veteran Albert Parsons, who, along with his wife, Lucy Parsons, had arrived in Chicago a few years earlier; they were already making names for themselves among both the working and ruling classes. More well-known were George Schilling and Paul Grottkau, who were also in attendance as members of labor's growing voice. No revolutionary changes came about as a result of the delegation's investigations. After the start of the twentieth century, in 1915, another legislative delegation from Springfield would investigate the conditions of labor in Chicago, but it would not be through legislative action that relief would be won.

By the middle of the 1880s, it was apparent to a growing number of Socialists that the liberation of the proletariat would only come through the hands of those who wielded the hammer and sickle, the age-old symbols of industry and agriculture. Tensions existed within the party as stalwarts of the political process continued in the vein of legislative action and electioneering. On March 26, 1884, in Seaman's Hall, near the present-day intersection of Randolph and Jefferson Streets, the Illinois Federation of Labor established committees to look into the issues of child and female labor, convict labor (as the state's cheap alternative to paying higher wages to those who were not convicts), workplace safety and sanitation, hours and wages/standard of living and the regulation of industry, namely the rail and telegraph lines.[23] Many were doubtful about the validity of more words and paper and resolutions and committees.

The city's original "Gold Coast" was to serve as a stage for the first major protest march against high society since the chaos of the 1877 national strikes. On Thanksgiving Day (November 27) in 1884, and again in 1885, the area served as the platform for the working people of Chicago to make their voices heard even as their stomachs rumbled, metaphorically and literally. Up and down Prairie Avenue south of Sixteenth Street, crowds of nearly 1,500 workers marched with red and black flags and banners reading "Bread or Work"—these men, women and children all had stories of their own that history books will never tell, and they all formed a mass pedestal for future workers and oppressed peoples who stand taller because of their actions.[24]

Between the two Thanksgiving Day marches, the Socialists gathered on April 28, 1885, at Market Square (now Wacker Drive in front of the Lyric Opera) for a protest rally and march against the dedication of the new building of the Chicago Board of Trade, located where LaSalle Street terminates into Jackson Boulevard (now the site of the 1930 Chicago Board of Trade Building). According to Chicago's *Daily Inter-Ocean*, about six hundred people peacefully (aside from a rock-throwing incident that resulted in a minor injury of one of the dedication attendees) marched from the square to the building and then back up Fifth Avenue (Wells Street) to the offices of the *Arbeiter-Zeitung* labor newspaper. It was from these offices that Albert Parsons and others gave statements to the press that would be used

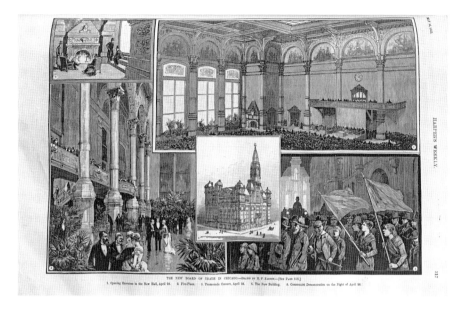

Harper's Weekly, on the 1885 dedication of the Chicago Board of Trade building, with the lower right corner acknowledgement of socialist protestors. *Courtesy of the Newberry Library and Nathanael Filbert.*

against them and result in their convictions for the Haymarket Riot and, by the end of 1887, the executions of four of them.[25]

By midsummer of 1885, the city sizzled in what turned out to be a low burn, ready to be ramped up during the monumental and tragic bombing the following May. The owners of the West Division Street Railway Company, which was not city-run at the time, exercised the oft-repeated capitalistic practice of ensuring profit by increasing rates for customers, cutting the wages of its workers (without the least reduction of executive salaries) and firing anyone who complained about any of it in the workplace. The month of July saw walkouts by laborers on the cars and in the car barns, the unhitching of horses from cars, the destruction of the cars and tracks that ran along the streets and the swarming of citizenry to support the workers. Strikebreakers (or "scabs," depending on your pleasure) were pulled from the train cars and beaten if they didn't voluntarily abandon their charges. Tracks were blocked, and a few were dynamited, all by people whose names will never be listed in official chronicles. These people, acting out of positions of powerlessness but acting in unison, became a formidable force that strong-armed city officials to plead with the streetcar company to negotiate a settlement.

The Statue of Industry (*left*) and Statue of Agriculture (*right*) that originally stood above the entrance to the 1885 Board of Trade building. *Courtesy of Nathanael Filbert and Brad Seifert.*

The Haymarket Memorial near Randolph and Desplaines Streets in the West Loop. *Courtesy of Nathanael Filbert and Brad Seifert.*

In the end, Mayor Carter Harrison, himself a recipient of some rocks thrown at him during the strike when he tried to calm down the crowds, was able to convince the company and workers to come to an agreement; by the end of July, the streetcars were running.[26]

One must keep in mind that by this time, the rotted, fetid condition of the election process had already pushed many Chicagoans away from the ballot box. Extremism rose within Socialist circles. Speeches became fiery, hope swelled for a new day of equity (and judgment) and plans developed for a vehicle to accomplish the revolution that would spread throughout the Western world.

The bombing at the Haymarket on the evening of May 4, 1886, needs to be assessed as the tragedy it was, both as an act of terror that killed civilians and police officers and as a usurping of the legal process to guarantee convictions and executions of people who dared challenge those in power. At a gathering that evening, socialists and workers heard speeches of protest against police violence from the previous day at a rally at the McCormick Reaper Works on the city's south side. While the third speech was being delivered, about 170 police officers approached, ordering the people to peacefully disperse. As Samuel Fielden got down from the makeshift dais, claiming the peacefulness of the proceedings, a bomb was thrown into the columns of police, killing Mathias Degan instantly. Eight men would eventually be convicted for his death and that of six other officers who died in the ensuing weeks; these eight men were charged with conspiracy to riot and commit murder.

But this was also an event that need not have happened if those in positions of power and wealth—lustily coveted by a few—had deigned to open up the political system and the treasure chests to make all people's lives more equitable. A workable socialism doesn't necessarily mean everybody having the same amount of everything, but it can mean that no one working with due diligence should have to scrape by with a subsistence wage (nefariously referred to as "minimum wage") that required, in the nineteenth and twentieth centuries, children as well as adults to work full-time and, today, people to work more than one job in order to barely survive. History has shown that there have been too few people in government who are true advocates of the poor and working classes when it comes to raising the standards of living for all.

It's good to pause here for a reflection on the role of religion, primarily Christianity, in the story of the Chicago worker and socialism. With the influx of Eastern and Southern European immigrants into the once solidly white Anglo-Saxon Protestant (WASP) United States came age-old tensions, primarily between Catholics and Protestants—one of them was the classic questioning of loyalty of the "papists" (Roman Catholics who are presumed to have a diehard allegiance to the Pope) to the American Dream. Sadly, for the American worker, U.S. prelates—bishops of the particular regions throughout the country—seemed to be more in favor of calm seas and unrocked boats; they seemed to ignore the memory of their Savior, who calmed rough waters and stayed the hands of wicked moneylenders.

These bishops were, at times, more American/capitalistic than they were devotees of the poor Jewish carpenter from Galilee who was born in a feedbox. These bishops and their Protestant counterparts tended to favor a quiet acceptance of the economic realities of the times in the hope of gaining eternal reward in the next life. Faith is well and good, and over the past several centuries, it has probably stayed the hand of many a Christian tyrant who would've acted more brutally against their brethren had they not held a healthy fear of eternal damnation. But holy wars, crusades and jihads aside, the fact remains that this faith-filled acceptance of existence had led to the departure of many from the churches and into the arms of the Socialists, who promised a "heaven on earth." The tensions between religion and socialism are only irreconcilable in that the expressed faith of the time went head to head against the promoters of social reconstruction; since the days of the French Revolution, churches have consistently been aligned with monarchs and colonialists, industrialists and capitalistic government.

By the end of the nineteenth century, there was a reawakening among a small number of church leaders and some of their flock. In 1891, Pope Leo XIII published *Rerum Novarum (On Capital and Labor)*, which literally translates to "On the New Things," the first major example of organized religion defining social responsibilities of capital and labor as a vehicle to a more just society. These ideas would be reiterated by Pope John Paul II in the *Centesimus Annus* (hundredth anniversary) encyclical. In the popular mind, Dorothy Day remains a major figure of the positive contributions of faith as related to the actions of an individual believer. There are other figures (again, out of the scope of this book), but the issue has been raised here to highlight the root of the tension between church and socialism. The Socialists consistently aligned themselves with the worker and principles of justice, and some had gone to the gallows for it, as the Nazarene had done.

After the Haymarket Riot, Chicago was a changed city in that those in power clung to the mechanisms that kept the social order in place. In the autumn, newspapers were filled with words chronicling the Democratic and Republican platforms for the national and state elections following the bombing and trial. Both parties condemned violence and upheld the maintenance of public order with a notable change of tone. While not giving in one iota on the necessity of law and order, at the same time, both parties strongly advocated harmony between the owners of businesses and the workers.[27]

Of course, these planks in the platforms in the ruling parties were repetitions of what the Socialists had been advocating for in Chicago for at least ten years. It may be the lot of humanity to undergo tumult prior to real social change, but it's a maddening proposition to witness the same behavior millennia after millennia, as the working class has done throughout recorded history—that the powerful will resist change until and only until that change is forced upon them.

Today, ours is not a culture that upholds reason and intellect but instead worships distraction through emotionalism, celebrity and scandal, so we fail to see the repetitiousness of history. The adage that history repeats itself is true, but not because the universe is an evil force that makes people go through the same trials over and over. It is repetitive because we lack the will to study it for solid understanding and to see patterns of human behavior—and misbehavior—in order to avoid the mistakes of the past.

May Day

Unemployment Parade & Mass Meeting!

Sunday, May 1st

**For Unemployment Insurance - - -
Against Starvation!
For a Shorter Workday - Against Exploitation!
For Peace - Against War!
For Socialism - Against Capitalism!**

JOIN THE PARADE!

Gathering Place: KEDZIE AND OGDEN AVES.
TIME: 1 p. m.

ROUTE: From Ogden and Kedzie west to Homan Ave. — On Homan Ave. north to Roosevelt Road — On Roosevelt Road east to Western Ave. —On Western Ave. north to Van Buren Street — On Van Buren Street east to Ashland Boulevard Auditorium for

THE MASS MEETING

Place: ASHLAND BOULEVARD AUDITORIUM,
corner Ashland Boulevard and Van Buren Street, at 3 P. M.

SPEAKERS:

Dr. J.B. MATTHEWS; Author, member of the faculties of Fisk University and Howard University, Teacher of a Chinese School in the Island of Java; Chairman of the First World Peace Conference in Holland in 1928 and of the First International Youth Leaders' Council in Germany in 1930.

ROY BURT; Socialist Party Candidate for Governor of Illinois; Well known Educator; Former Miner in Southern Illinois.

KARL BORDERS; Secretary of the League for Industrial Democracy; Chairman of the Workers Committee on Unemployment; Candidate on the County Ticket of the Farmer Labor Party.

DR. R. B. GREEN; Prominent Physician in Chicago; Farmer Labor Party Candidate for Coroner of Cook County.

HYMAN SCHNEID; From the Amalgamated Clothing Workers of America; Socialist Party Candidate for Congressman at Large.

ADOLPH DREIFUSS; Secretary of the Socialist Party of Cook County; Socialist Party Candidate for Secretary of State of Ill.

Also speakers of Paole Zion and other Federations.

SUBJECT:

Unemployment and Economic and Political Demands of the Masses!

WORKMEN CIRCLE CHORUS AND
GERMAN WORKERS SINGING SOCIETY.

A nominal admission fee of 10c only will be charged to help defray expenses.

Workingmen and Workingwomen, show your strength and stand up for your class!

MAY DAY CONFERENCE
Representing Socialist and Labor Organizations.

561 Socialist Party Center, 3036 Roosevelt Rd., Phone Kedzie 4316

A Socialist broadside announcing a May Day meeting, circa 1930. *Courtesy of the Chicago History Museum* (CHM: i019694).

We're condemned to repeat our past because, in the present, we choose to focus our energies on analyzing the tweets of self-absorbed and overpaid athletes, movie stars and politicians. These are the American royals—the ones whose lives are chronicled by the minute by followers who digitally stalk their moves, random thoughts and pettiness.

However, celebrity status is not a beast in and of itself—it's created by an audience, and all bear the responsibility of the blood of the sacrificed. Excessive salaries are not only socially unjust because they usually come from the labor of people who share only a fraction of the profits but also because an astronomical amount of money has a corrosive effect on the individual. One only has to observe the stories of countless celebrities who gain massive incomes at a young age or adults who win a lottery with a prize that equals some nations' gross national products. This glorification of material wealth seemingly has no limit, as this culture constantly obsesses over its "haves" and ignores its "have-nots."

This is a culture in which the American ruling aristocracy perpetuates itself by dating, marrying and procreating within its own stratum (much like centuries of royals have done). They can jet off to Venice for dinner to satisfy a craving for Italian food while proletariat children all over the country need a public school to provide something nutritious in their stomachs in the morning. This is a culture in which parents feel powerless, compelled to run their children ragged through incessant athletic competitions at the expense of leisure time with the goal of their progeny attaining capitalistic success via free money for college (totally understandable) or piles of cash in professional sports. Just as nineteenth-century parents were forced to pimp their children to business owners in order for the family to survive, so, too, do modern-day guardians feel compelled, with the looming specter of college debt, to find additional sources of revenue. The economic system creates the beast, and none but the staunchest gladiator can stand against it.

And once again, we're ignoring the looming monstrosity, just as the political and economic bosses in Chicago turned away from the growing poverty in the city in the last quarter of the nineteenth century. Today, the disparity between rich (let's say, those who got invited to the British royal wedding in 2018) and the working class and poor (those who had to clean up after it, or those who have to clean up every day after American royals do whatever it is they do) is growing. The inability of the ruling political parties—at the local, state and national levels—to rationally address the issues without resorting to mudslinging and temper tantrums demonstrates their abject impotence and incompetence, yet they continue to be reelected.

The tragedy is that most of the citizenry seem to accept the political game, knowing that the rules of said game are written so as to guarantee the perpetuation of the game as it has always been played. Politicians who are somehow admired for their "public service" for fifty years in the Chicago City Council and Springfield Legislature and notorious for their actions that favor their own clients in the private sector (with ramifications for the people in the public sphere) are consistently reelected while consistently garnering the support of the political machine against the interests of the people, the ones who are most consistently fleeced and who, the politicians know, will consistently vote to keep them in power. These same people—the children of the ostracized generations of the past—are continually manipulated and baited with promises, slogans and paltry handouts from the banquet table of those in power in this city.

The Fourteenth Ward, once a strong bloc of socialist voters, has been in the hands of the Democratic Party and machine gameplaying at the expense of the largely Latino population. As of this writing, its alderman, Edward Burke, having completed his fifth decade in city hall, is under federal investigation; his real estate tax business has been very successful, allegedly thanks to some exertion of muscle against small franchise owners; and he has reaped some benefit while in office and finagling big-fish deals by netting $14 million in tax breaks for the downtown Trump Tower—a building owned by the man who would build a wall to try to keep out many of Burke's constituents.

For those who resist the droning of the mechanisms of the machine or dare support reform-minded leaders, they can, more often than not, expect to feel a kickback—and not the kind associated with financial benefit. In Chicago, anecdotal stories abound of snap inspections, closings of small businesses, fines based on outdated city code books that have been dusted off to use against anyone daring to support someone other than the politically baptized. One only has to stroll about the city and take a look into shop windows during municipal election time. A complete list of aldermen/women ("aldermaniacs," for gender neutral purposes) can be garnered by a visit to each ward and a stop at a bar or restaurant. Only the most stalwart business owner can dare post a handbill in favor of an incumbent's opponent, as has been witnessed by this author in certain machine-infested wards.

As long as ward bosses have an almost regal presence among their constituents, conditions will remain the same—the outcast citizen will continue to grovel at the feet of the reigning politicians and their nobility in city hall; the well-connected will continue to pay their tribute and reap the benefits of the open treasure chest that has always been within their grasp.

As long as Chicago continues with its "nonpartisan" elections, featuring a candidate list without party affiliation, those in power will remain in power. The machine will continue to churn out safe candidates who will become safe public officials who work to perpetuate the process. The ruling class will continue to rule and reap the benefits of reigning over a deluded population.

As of the initial writing of this draft, the municipal elections on February 26, 2019, promised to be colorful, if nothing else: sixteen candidates were vying for the executive spot in the city, all promising change. With much verbiage about reform, eleven of those seeking the office of mayor had previous work in electioneering, city and county government and access to the most connected channels of power. It seemed less likely that a strong reformist candidate would rise and more in the realm of the probable that a familiar hand would snatch the reins of power, and the voters of Chicago would kowtow to a familiar name, marching to an all-too-familiar beat from a winking band of players.

One "bright light" in the "Hall of Political Debauch" that is the seedier side of Chicago politics is, to some extent, the result of the 2019 municipal elections. Sadly, only a third (around 33 percent) of registered voters exercised their right to the ballot; in spite of this, six Democratic Socialists won seats in the city council. The voters of the First, Twentieth, Twenty-Fifth, Thirty-Third, Thirty-Fifth and Fortieth Wards sent clear messages to those enthroned; respectively, they are Daniel Laspata, Jeanette Taylor, Bryon Sigcho-Lopez, Rossana Rodriguez, Carlos Ramirez-Rosa and Andre Vasquez, all of whom were listed as members of the Democratic Socialists of America party on the Chicago Election website (www.chicagoelections.com) as of this writing. A perusal of the results shows that twenty-seven incumbents won outright (including Edward Burke, who is under federal investigation for extortion), and fifteen were forced into a runoff in which six of them lost their positions.

The question needs to be raised about the possibility of ongoing reform in the power structure of city government when so few citizens vote—what would have happened with 50 or 75 percent voter turnout? Chicago now has a mayor—Lori Lightfoot—who won not because of her color, gender or sexual orientation but because of her program of reform and openness. It was a clear message sent by a minority of people; Lightfoot won about three-quarters of the votes from the 33 percent who voted—not a landslide, by any means, but perhaps the start of the cracking of the rusted mechanisms of codified political narcissism.

Chapter 4

THE ROLLING TIDE: PORTERS, JOURNALISTS AND THE WEAK SPOTS AT THE DAWN OF THE TWENTIETH CENTURY

Come senators, congressmen/Please heed the call/Don't stand in the doorway/ Don't block up the hall/For he that gets hurt/Will be he who has stalled/There's a battle outside and it is ragin'/It'll soon shake your windows and rattle your walls/For the times they are a-changin'.[28]
—*Bob Dylan*

If there's one point where socialism has been most consistent and others have misunderstood, it's regarding the issue of equity. As stated in the previous chapter, it is not about everything being the same and everyone getting everything in the exact amounts as everyone else. Equity is fairness, impartiality and justice, according to *Webster's Dictionary*. To provide a minimum understanding in relation to economic principle, it should be expressed as just compensation of wages for labor given.

During the Great Railroad Strike of 1877, Albert Parsons (among several others who were not as notorious as Albert and his wife, Lucy) tried to unmask the brutality of the economic system that spawned the upheaval of that time—the railroad owners' fixing of wages and defining the value of labor while "the worker is bound hand and foot" and therefore is "a slave" working twelve to fifteen hours per day for a fraction of the profit. In the same vein, as reported in the *Chicago Tribune*, "All hands felt hard towards the railroad company because they had reduced the poorest paid workingmen and left the President, Managers, supervisors and foremen alone."[29]

The Socialist became the consistent voice of the worker in Chicago during this period. Calvin A. Light, an editor for the *Indianapolis Times*, expressed basic socialistic principles while at a labor demonstration in West Belleville, Illinois; his editorial was picked up and published in Chicago. "[I]f your 20,000 workmen…receive $2.00 per day…$40,000 for all, while they create three times that amount…you cannot with your $40,000 buy $120,000 worth of goods. [You have] a glut in the market…so-called over-production, which is really under-consumption."[30] Josephine Conger-Kaneko would echo this in her journals on the eve of World War I. Walter Hurt, writing in the *Coming Nation*, condemned "the inequitable distribution of products and an unequal distribution of labor: some men work inordinate hours while others starve in idleness."[31]

Extending this theme in the same issue in which Hurt's article was printed and in the same vein of sarcasm that would fuel Chicago's leftist voice, an anonymous writer stated:

> *The capitalist class are fond of benevolence to the deserving needy. Only they take great care that the needy should really deserve benevolence.…We on our part must grant that this principle is just. (No support of "sloth, indolence, beggary and crime") Let us apply this universally! There is in the U.S., paid out annually, a sum of $2,000 million* [$2 billion in 1878, which translates, roughly, to about $50 trillion in 2018], *in the shape of dividends.*[32]

In the United States, the fifty years after the Civil War were full of economic turmoil as a result of the war, the Reconstruction era in the former Confederacy and the beginning of a massive wave of African American migration from the South as well as European immigration that would not slow in Chicago until the eve of World War II.[33] The swell of workers provided industrialists with an overflowing pool from which to draw workers, and it was an owner's market: worker was pitted against worker, especially during economic downturns, in a competition to see who would work for the lowest wages. Racial and ethnic tensions increased. On November 11, 1879, a *Chicago Tribune* editorial stated that M.W. Wheeler wired San Francisco for fifty Chinese workers to come to Chicago.[34] The stage was being set for a rabid attack against Asians that would engulf the American labor movement in general and the Socialist Party of Chicago in particular.

By the time the dynamite was thrown at the Haymarket in 1886, the United States had been steaming ahead with increased power for a quarter of a century in spite of periodic economic downturns. What had been a largely agrarian-based economy from the time of the American Revolution was changed four generations later with thunderous effect. Wage-earners in Chicago whose grandparents may have been farmers on the East Coast or in Europe knew only of long hours in stockyards, garment mills, and lumber and rail yards. Rather than smell the natural odors of the planet, as their forebears had done, men, women and children inhaled the stench of decaying flesh, chemicals and burning coal. This fueled a socialism that sought "to ameliorate the devasting excesses which rapid industrialization had wrought on the urban poor."[35]

The strike became the strongest defense for the worker, though it had its flaws. For a strike to be successful, it has to be universal in terms of participation. Any member not forged in the fire of conviction that theirs is a just struggle represents a crack in the cup of fraternity. Owners of business knew this, as they hired substitutes for their striking workers—sometimes paying them less than their out-of-work comrades—and sowed seeds of discord among the laboring class, often playing on racial and ethnic tensions that were already present.

Striking worker and police officer during the 1904 Stockyard Strike in Chicago. *Courtesy of the Chicago History Museum.*

The Pullman Strike of 1894 was the first major labor action in Chicago since the 1886 May Day strikes, rallies and bombing. Bigger than the strike of the previous year, which threatened the opening of the World's Fair on the south side, the Pullman Strike would bring in national socialist leadership (under Eugene Debs) as well as the crushing hand of the federal government (through the pen of President Grover Cleveland).

In September 1893, the Pullman Company had ordered a reduction in wages of nearly 25 percent. In the famed "Pullmantown," the worker residence and brainchild of owner George Pullman (now the Chicago neighborhood of the same name), there was no concurrent lowering of rents or utilities. And, yet again, there was no comparable reduction in the salaries of management or owners or in the dividends paid out to stockholders.[36]

The passenger cars of the Pullman Company were staffed by porters and other railway workers—conductors, brakemen and so on. Prior to the May 11 walkout, there were several firings of workers who had advocated for unionization. According to company personnel books, from the end of March 1894 to the beginning of the strike in the middle of May, dozens of men were let go in the Chicago section of the company.[37] Now, granted,

Pullmantown, 1890. *Courtesy of the Chicago History Museum.*

people can be discharged for a variety of justifiable reasons, but in the two-month period mentioned above, over one hundred men were fired in Chicago alone. There are simply names in a massive ledger book with dates of termination inscribed next to them. It was the dismissals of committee members who had expressed the desire to meet with company officials that provided the immediate cause for the strike.

From May 11 until August 2, when the strike officially ended, Chicago was center stage for an end-of-the-century clash between capital and labor. Debs and other leaders in Chicago were arrested in the second week of July after defying a federal injunction against the strike. (President Cleveland had ordered that mail cars be attached to the passenger cars, thereby making the strike a criminal action that interfered with the U.S. Postal Service.) Federal troops had been dispatched on July 3. By July 12, it was clear that the American Federation of Labor would not order sympathetic strikes from other unions in other industries across the country to support the Chicagoans, and the Pullman Strike died of strangulation on August 2.[38]

Economic instability was the norm in the decades following the Civil War, and it was this turmoil that contributed to the labor unrest in Chicago. The growing railroad industry—upon which industrialists depended to ship their goods across the country—saw stagnation in the 1880s. Chicago, being the "Hog Butcher to the World," according to Carl Sandburg, was hit with particular force. The Chicago Board of Trade suffered under a decade of decline of the price of packed beef and pork that began in 1891. From 1885 to 1900, Chicago stagnated as the six major rail lines running through the city increased shipments of flour, wheat, corn and other agricultural commodities by a mere 1.6 million bushels; this increase was small considering the average annual shipping business of about 60 million bushels.[39]

It is fair to point out that in times of economic bouncing, the times are good for a fair number of people—merchants, owners of business and other industrial magnates, as well as the working class. It also needs to be clarified that bad economic times are particularly hurtful for the poor and the laboring masses. Even as major economic depressions wreak havoc on owners as well as workers, and there are examples of people losing life savings or investments in times of industrial collapse, the lower economic classes experience the blow crashing down the hardest.

In the winter of 1909, Chicago's Josephine Conger-Kankeko wrote in her newborn publication, the *Socialist Woman*:

[T]*here was so much poverty, so much misery. And they who owned the coal mines, they who owned the money, they who owned the jobs, sat in their cushioned pews and chanted mechanically, 'Lord, have mercy upon us, miserable offenders.....But the freezing poor, walking the streets and slinking away from the windward side of the great churches, ground their teeth in the bitterness of their hearts, and with the Man of Galilee denounced the whited sepulchers within.*[40]

"Centennials" in Chicago, like today's "millennials" (the people born at the beginning and end of the turn of a century), came into the Windy City around 1900 during a biting cold in the working-class neighborhoods. With most adult workers earning between twenty-two and fifty cents per hour (with female garment workers at the lowest and male bricklayers at the highest ends of the wage rate) and working an average of eight to ten hours per day, the universal education of children became more difficult, and these children also had to go to work in order for the family to avoid starvation. Farmworkers throughout the state of Illinois saw similar destitution, with an average monthly wage, including board, of about thirty dollars. This breaks down to about one dollar and twenty-five cents per day, or twelve cents an hour for a ten-hour day on a farm.[41]

Farmworkers outside Barrington, Illinois, 1929. *Courtesy of the Chicago History Museum.*

The cultural assumption that has lamely justified lower wages for women does not seem to be founded in the experience of the working class; the popular myth that men have historically made more money than women because they were the main source of income for their families doesn't coincide with reality. It was because wages were so low and neither parent could support a household on a single wage that both adults in a typical family had to work in this era. Now, if one is talking about an executive or an owner of business, then it seems understandable to view the man's sole earnings as being sufficient to support a family—understandable, but not necessarily justifiable. The historical record is what it is, and the titans of industry made enough so that their wives didn't have to work outside the home for economic reasons, unlike those who helped create the wealth the industrialists and their families enjoyed.

Around this same time, Mayor Carter Harrison the second, son of the first mayor of that name (again, no coincidence), earned a salary of $10,000 per year, or $32 per day for a six-day week.[42] In 1907, Mayor Fred Busse earned $18,000 per year, or $57.50 per day.[43] Granted, these are not exorbitant amounts, but the disparity between these incomes and that of the average citizen is evident.

Today, inequity is the cause of social ills much as it was at the time Conger-Kaneko wrote and published. Basic socialist principle is rooted in this reality. When Chicagoans were riding the waves of economic bounty and destitution, Algie Martin Simons, editor of the Chicago-based *International Socialist Review*, wrote of it but based it in the abject inequality demonstrated by the propertied class of the late eighteenth century in the North and South of the newly independent United States versus the immigrating working class and kidnapped Africans:

> *In the North, immigration supplied the ruling classes with unlimited quantities of labor power in a cheap form, and it soon became evident that wage slavery was by far cheaper* [cheaper than chattel slavery, the slavery of the South, in which slave owners had to pay for the "upkeep" of their slaves].…*Today* [1903] *it takes half a million men to harvest, transport and prepare a loaf of bread. Yet two or three men may own all the means with which the work is done, and that ownership enables them to enslave the half million who do the work.*[44]

The sweeping industrialization of the nineteenth century had borne fruit for property and factory owners. Land grants, as well as government wartime production contracts, enabled the propertied few to further benefit. The average worker could do nothing but submit to contract labor, which, in reality, was nothing of the sort—a contract implies equality and mutual benefit. A worker agreed to a fixed wage set by the owner, and it was nonnegotiable. It's good to note here that with the presence of unions, the worker can be assisted in balancing the agreement.

Through the start of the twentieth century, the worker was still at a disadvantage. By this time, a generation before Henry Ford would perfect the concept of the assembly line, workers no longer made whole products and certainly had no hand in selling the merchandise, as artisans and laborers had done in previous generations. Laborers sold their time at the going rate in the marketplace. "Wage slave" became their moniker in a society that rooted the rights of life, liberty and the pursuit of happiness in the ownership of property that brought the possessors of said property a profit.[45] This practice, along with its attending social acceptance, has had disastrous effect in the social order for the members of the working class, from the oldest to the youngest.

Since the 1870s, socialists had championed the end of child labor, and in the new century, Conger-Kaneko recognized the need for universal education for children and adults, especially women, as essential to the party's platform and as the key to social reform. In the *Coming Nation*, the third incarnation of her socialistic journal, she published an article by John M. Work on capitalism, the enemy of the family. He voiced the main leftist argument (the *real* leftist argument, not the faux one trumpeted by the modern-day Democratic Party) in favor of reform. In the article, he placed the blame for the social ills of prostitution, low wages, child labor and illiteracy, overwork and poverty squarely on the shoulders of big business.[46] Echoing this sentiment as a strong advocate of dismantling the social structures that kept most of the population in poverty and ignorance, Algie Simons speaks as a relevant voice from the past to contemporary ears:

> [L]*ines of a new class struggle are being drawn. Upon the one side stand all the workers, with hand or with brain, from the field, the factory and the office, driven together by the same exploiting force. Opposed to these stands a little handful of men, growing ever smaller in number, even greater in power, who hold the destiny of the world in their hands. These men control the press, the lecture platforms, the great universities, the schools and all the means by which public opinion is made and controlled.*[47]

To counter this argument, businessmen of the time claimed that their individual rights of ownership gave them a freedom to negotiate for lowest cost just as the free market dictates the overall cost of commodities. "Private business is private business" became the cheer—amplifying the idea that wages were a private matter to be protected from outside interference. In the words of Charles Yerkes, who was the president of the Union Iron and Steel Company during a pre-Haymarket labor dispute in Chicago, "Sooner than allow my company to be dictated to by a crowd of men under the leadership of Socialists and Anarchists, I will discharge everyone on the road."[48]

Ultimately, the socialist struggle for equity is centered on the ability of all people to have an equal opportunity for a fruitful life. This is accomplished through education, just wages and an equal voice in the running of society in order to better enjoy the fruits of an organized and peaceful world. There is nothing revolutionary in these expectations, but it is tragic that over the decades and throughout the world, people have had to rise up to achieve these basic human needs. The twentieth-century struggle in Chicago brought to light the growing realization that worker solidarity was essential as it took on an increasingly polychromatic and multiethnic stance in the early decades.

Socialism would aid in the increased sense of the universality of the struggle. The Knights of Labor, one of the earliest union bodies in Chicago (and, in the early 1880s, the most supported in socialist circles), fully supported membership for any worker despite color or creed; the platform was broad enough to take in all.[49] The voice of the Knights would be greatly weakened and reduced to a whisper in the aftermath of the 1886 Haymarket Riot. The group would limp into the twentieth century and eventually be absorbed, for the most part, by the newly risen and more socially acceptable American Federation of Labor (AFL).

Now, it also should be pointed out that although the early labor movement was theoretically all-embracing, the ugly reality of human shortfall (even among socialists) is that, at times, fear dictated action in union circles. African American workers were heartily employed by owners and strongly supported by unions, but "color prejudice is used like any other weapon to strengthen the monopoly of the labor unions."[50] Business owners would bring in workers and "strategically drew lines [of wage, color and gender] separating, and in the wake of strikes and walk-outs, effectively reorganized the service market."[51] At the same time, the Chinese Exclusion Act of 1882, the Alien Contract Labor Law (Foran Act) of 1885 and the Immigration Act (Literary Test Act) of 1917 all played on passionate xenophobia to protect "American jobs."

As it is good for Christians to remember that Jesus picked Judas Iscariot to be a follower who would later betray him, so should socialists never forget that society is made up of everyone, and the full story isn't always beautiful. The core flaw of Marxism is that the class struggle has focused too much on a "we versus they" dialectic. The human story is the story of a people struggling to share the bounty of the one planet on which we all live. One of the avenues out of the contentious atmosphere we have at present, in 2019, is built on seeing commonalities over differences. A single issue that exemplifies this is world trade.

Healthy trade relationships among the collective nations of the world is a good that only strengthens each individual country and the people who live in them. It must be restated that socialism is rooted in the belief of the fraternity of the human race—that to employ anyone is in the best interest of everyone, that an injury to one is an injury to all, that the denial of rights of an individual endangers the rights of the whole. While supporting a worker on the other side of the world by buying a product made on another continent, one is supporting a trade and market strategy that is global and can therefore be beneficial to one and all.

More basic to the average worker is the issue of wages. Like the debate about an eight-hour workday in the nineteenth century, today's "Fight For $15" is the current hallmark of worker rights. And much like the main argument against the eight-hour day, the fifteen-dollars-per-hour minimum wage proposal is contested by predicting doom in terms of small businesses and consumer prices. These are legitimate fears—that first generation of workers who demanded the reduction of the workday from ten (sometimes more) to eight hours were also demanding pay raises based on their regular ten-hour workdays. Of course, one can imagine the reaction of the business owners and economic pundits of the time. The fact is that over time, the market stabilized, prices did not skyrocket and, in the end, the American worker has received more money to spend and more time in which to spend it. This last point, by the way, was the consistent socialist argument in favor of the eight-hour workday. "Eight hours to work, eight hours to rest and eight hours to do whatever we please" was the adage of the early labor movement.

So, today, it is reasonable to expect that over a short period of time (a few years), the minimum wage in the United States can be raised to fifteen dollars per hour without the economic chaos predicted by the reigning philosophies of industry. Of course, it is reasonable to assume that there will be some need for price adjustments to make up for such a dramatic increase.

As has happened over the past 125 years, adjustments will come as workers gain more money in their pockets and acquire more time during which to spend it—especially if the minimum wage allows them and their families to live in relative comfort with one job. This has already been made visible in Chicago, as the minimum wage was increased to thirteen dollars per hour on July 1, 2019; merchants have posted signage explaining that increases in prices have been made to offset the raise in wages of its workers (these increases are modest in most businesses in the city as compared to the sticker shock of gas prices that spike whenever someone on Wall Street belches).

Economic inequity is evident in our own day, as some who live in comfort look down not only on the unemployed but also on those who work in certain sectors of the economy—ask anyone in foodservice, retail or education. Ask anyone else *not* in these sectors while there's a strike going on for a raise in the hourly rate or for full health coverage or protection of teacher pensions. This economy pays out—and this culture perpetuates the paying out of—the minimum amount of a barely-living wage, so many workers (including teachers) have to double up on jobs, while professional athletes and entertainers rake in obscene pay. Economic justice will be served when athletes have to pay for their own equipment to do their jobs while teachers get paid a salary commensurate with their tasks.

Even more importantly, economic justice will be served when state and city governments stop using tax money to fund the efforts of team owners and studio executives in the construction of "bigger and better" stadiums and movie sets in particular locales. Equity will be strengthened when these multimillionaires who pay out exorbitant salaries to athletes, musicians and actors are blocked from receiving massive tax breaks through the federal government and "creative accounting."

The shock of increased wages is at the level it is because Democrats and Republicans have refused to act with the interests of the worker in mind and have refused to raise the federal minimum wage (seven dollars and twenty-five cents per hour, as of summer 2019) for over ten years. This number sets the lowest level—the floor, as it were—that wages can be set in the U.S. workplace. How many industrialists, bankers and legislators would be willing to live on seven dollars and twenty-five cents per hour (without their bonuses, stock options, pensions and severance packages), and do our elected officials think of this reality as they vote to give themselves pay raises?

Fear-mongering, like the above-mentioned doomsday predictions by the economically advantaged, has consistently stirred opposition to basic improvements in the living conditions of the "lower classes." The idle rich

Mayor Edward Kelly (*right*) and boxing legend Joe Louis in a pose symbolic of the machine's manipulation of Chicago voters. *Courtesy of the Chicago History Museum.*

seem to protest most strongly against those deemed to be noncontributing members of society; those who extend their hands to the government for special tax concessions and contracts are quick to smack down the hands of those who are seeking a lift up and out of their condition of servitude. The socialist principle of equity must be remembered—everyone doesn't need the same amount of everything, but everyone does deserve an equal opportunity to satisfy the basic human needs of comfort in the modern world.

Democrats will freely support programs for the poor and the worker as long as those same poor and working people allow themselves to be kept on a leash and beholden to the political bosses dangling the carrots in front of them. Republicans will condescend to grant certain social concessions as long as business interests are protected and economic disparity remains more or less intact. Both parties will connive with each other and with business interests to keep the status quo static.

And the electorate continues to keep them in office—business as usual, as the adage says. As long as we continue to accept screaming matches in place of debates, substitute arguments via memes for rational discourse and read or listen to news sources and blogs that only support our own narrow opinions, we will not experience a change in leadership or in the health of this republic.

Chapter 5

POLITICIANS AND REFORMERS: MAP OF DISASTER OR BLUEPRINT FOR PEACE?

Who are the Socialists? [They] *demand the free birthright of all…to the access of nature's bounty by means of their own labor, they strive to reconstruct society so that no* [one] *needs to depend upon another's means for the privilege of making a proper use of* [their] *God-given working-strength harvesting the fruits therefore all for* [themselves].[52]
—*Editorial in* The Socialist, *1878*

The socialists of early-twentieth-century Chicago were able to harness the energy of a large number of people of various backgrounds despite the inherent tension of forging a unified movement out of such diversity. In addition to accommodating the growing number of freed slaves and first-generation freeborn men and women migrating from the southern states, as well as the Northern European immigrants of the previous seventy-five years, the city was making room for the wave of newcomers from Eastern Europe and the Mediterranean basin.

This challenge—a glut in the workforce due to the influx of workers—was identified in the previous generation by Carroll D. Wright, the first commissioner of the U.S. Bureau of Labor. In March 1886, in the "First Annual Report of the Commission of Labor," Wright observed that "the increase in immigration means an increase in the labor supply, therefore lower wages and overproduction, crippling consuming power of the whole."[53]

From 1880 to 1890, Chicago had grown from having a population of 503,000 to just over 1 million, with foreign-born residents increasing from just under 205,000 to 450,000. By 1900, Chicago's population had grown to almost 1.7 million, with immigrant residents accounting for nearly 600,000 of that number. In ten years, the city would be home to about 2.2 million, with immigrants accounting for 783,000 of the total number.[54] All came for work, a better life, opportunity, wealth and a host of other reasons—and this brought inherent conflict, at times.

The workshops of the garment industry became one of the strongest areas of socialist activity. Long hours, low pay, child labor, "piecework" at home as well as appalling conditions in the workplace contributed to a massive effort to organize workers and force change.[55] Jewish workers, many of whom had roots in Eastern Europe, became vocal advocates of reform. Sidney Hillman and Bessie Abramowitz were the most recognizable in the city. They, along with a number of nameless women, were instrumental in the 1910 garment workers' strike, which was sparked by yet another announced wage cut. On September 22, the spontaneous walkout of sixteen women from the Hart, Schaffner and Marx Company began a five-month standoff between ownership and workers. It would grow to a massive movement of forty thousand garment workers, 80 percent of them of Jewish heritage.[56] A settlement was reached in early 1911; work resumed, union members' jobs were assured and an arbitration committee was established.

The cost of goods related to the garment industry can be discovered by reading any of the hundreds of advertisements in the city's newspapers of the day. A sale on various items made clothing and other apparel a little more affordable to the working class that manufactured them: adult shoes were offered for 98¢; women's suits, regularly selling for $20, went for $4.75, while a woman's coat sold for $12.75; men's suits sold for $10; school suits for boys and girls averaged about $1.85; and a wool blanket, an absolute winter necessity, sold for $5.75.[57] A reminder from the previous chapter—garment workers, especially female employees, were on the lowest rung of the wage ladder, earning under 25¢ per hour, and some made significantly less.

In 1913, a state senatorial committee chaired by Niels Juul, along with Lieutenant Governor Barratt O'Hara, was established to investigate wages and working conditions in Chicago's garment district. Among those interviewed by the state officials was a thirty-six-year-old woman of Russian descent with three children. She worked at a place—unnamed

Garment workers after the resolution of the 1915 strike in Chicago. *Courtesy of the Chicago History Museum.*

due to her fear of employer retribution—on Jefferson and Twelfth Streets (Roosevelt Road) for five days each week from 7:30 a.m. until 6:00 p.m. for three dollars and forty cents per week (sixty-eight cents per day, or six cents per hour). Her husband made nine dollars each week.[58] Through the course of several individual testimonies, it was discovered by the committee that a third of the employees were paid less than eight dollars per week, the recognized "bread-line" (now called the poverty line). Juul recommended that those who testified before the committee be given one dollar apiece to compensate them for their time as well as the assumed dockage of their pay by employers for having missed work in order to appear.[59]

While admirable and heartening, the words of the committee were stronger than the resulting legislative action. Government intervention was not forthcoming in any significant way at the time. Major labor action would be necessary, and strikes were repeated in this industry in Chicago in 1915 and 1916.

The story of the African American experience in the socialist movement follows a similar pattern yet is unique in the lack of strength with which that group was welcomed into the party itself and the integrated labor movement. Basic socialist doctrine sees the issue of this experience first and foremost in terms of economics.

A strongly worded presentation was given in Gary, Indiana, at the first gathering of the Black Workers Congress in 1971. It formulated essentially three economic causes, based in a Marxist historical perspective, as the impetus for the three-hundred-year slave trade in the United States. First, the demand of the thirteen colonies along the Atlantic coast of North America for "black labor" was fueled by the desire to accumulate wealth and establish economic independence from the British Empire. Second, it allowed for the solidification of social status and hid the reality of class division in the newly formed democracy after the American Revolution. And, finally, it allowed "for greater manipulation of white workers than those workers normally would have accepted by the ruling class if there were no 'niggers' [sic] to look down upon in condescension and fear."[60]

In turn-of-the-century Chicago, racism, segregation and economic disparity had similar effects on housing and employment opportunities. Sadly, many leaders of the labor movement at this time upheld the age-old practices:

> [In 1896], *many Chicago labor leaders would affirm the racial hierarchies imposed by industrial foremen and their employers, making it almost impossible for black workers to align with white. Racial barriers in the workplace, reinforced by racial segregation in the city's neighborhoods, stamped out workers' belief in mutual, biracial support.*[61]

An uneasy accommodation existed in various industries in Chicago with regard to African American workers prior to World War I. The black population in Chicago in 1910 was about 44,000.[62] By 1920, that number had risen (mostly in the late 1910s) to 109,000 as a result of the "Great Migration" that offered the promise of a better life in the urban centers of the Midwest than those in the rural South. This population increase, as well as the influx of thousands of discharged soldiers after Armistice Day in 1918, would stoke the fires of racism and violence in Chicago. The First World War, the war "to end all wars," resulted in about 2.75 million individuals from the United States, black and white, being drafted in the year and a half of U.S. involvement. After the German/Austro-Hungarian surrender, more than one million soldiers were discharged and returned to civilian life in this country.[63]

As often happens, war brings economic prosperity (at least to those who chalk one up in the win column), while usually, in its wake, a downturn in fortune is not far behind. Those who answered the call of politicians and celebrities to defeat the "Huns" left their jobs, while others picked up the employment. After some semblance of peace was restored across the Atlantic, those million-plus returning veterans expected their old jobs to be available to them.

In all fairness, as the war was coming to a close, the state legislature in Springfield anticipated the need for greater economic opportunities for the working class on the south side of Chicago. In mid-October 1918, the Illinois Council for Defense established a commission to survey the transportation facilities of Chicago's southern section and into the northwest Indiana steel mill district to Gary.[64] The commission admitted that from Hyde Park to Bronzeville, from Sixty-Third Street to Thirty-First Street, the running times of the trains were too long for the convenience of the workers.[65] The commission's recommendations sought to increase the number of stops (in late 1918, this was already in progress) between Chicago and Gary, the number of trains running (in order to coincide with workers' schedules) and the number of streetcars in Gary; extend the mileage of tracks and create a double-track system to improve service; and add to the number of cars in each train run.[66]

Government action within the railroad industry had been a standard plank in the Socialist Party's platform since 1876, but it was only during wartime and its aftermath that the necessity of such intervention was realized by those in control. This, of course, did not lead to the nationalization of the rail system in the United States, as had been called for by the Socialists, but even in our own day, it does stand as an example of the necessity of systemic change (if only incremental) to achieve overall improvements in the livelihood of the working class.

The "Red Summer" that raged from May through August 1919 in many states was spawned by the aforementioned postwar economic downturn and glut in the labor market in addition to the already strongly developed racism throughout the country. By the end of July, Chicago found itself among the list of cities consumed by the violence following the murder of Eugene Williams, an African American youth guilty of nothing more than drifting into a "whites only" portion of Lake Michigan near Twenty-First Street. The actions of the police department, which included arresting a black lifeguard

Memorial plaque near the Twenty-First Street beach, the location of Eugene Williams's murder. *Courtesy of Nathanael Filbert.*

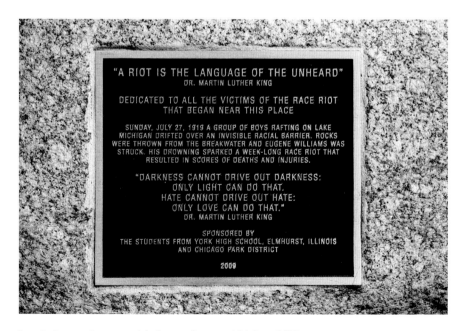

"A RIOT IS THE LANGUAGE OF THE UNHEARD"
DR. MARTIN LUTHER KING

DEDICATED TO ALL THE VICTIMS OF THE RACE RIOT
THAT BEGAN NEAR THIS PLACE

SUNDAY, JULY 27, 1919 A GROUP OF BOYS RAFTING ON LAKE
MICHIGAN DRIFTED OVER AN INVISIBLE RACIAL BARRIER. ROCKS
WERE THROWN FROM THE BREAKWATER AND EUGENE WILLIAMS WAS
STRUCK. HIS DROWNING SPARKED A WEEK-LONG RACE RIOT THAT
RESULTED IN SCORES OF DEATHS AND INJURIES.

"DARKNESS CANNOT DRIVE OUT DARKNESS:
ONLY LIGHT CAN DO THAT.
HATE CANNOT DRIVE OUT HATE:
ONLY LOVE CAN DO THAT."
DR. MARTIN LUTHER KING

SPONSORED BY
THE STUDENTS FROM YORK HIGH SCHOOL, ELMHURST, ILLINOIS
AND CHICAGO PARK DISTRICT

2009

Inscription on the memorial plaque. *Courtesy of Nathanael Filbert.*

who identified the white killer, as well as city officials' initial inaction led to two weeks of murder, destruction and intensified resentments among black and white Chicagoans.

Across the country, the political system reacted in much the same fashion: violence begets violence until the violence is stopped—and more often than not, "stopping" it results in more violence. Violence would spring forward again and again in the race riots of 1943 and again in 1968 following the assassination of Dr. Martin Luther King Jr. It has been a sad legacy that has continued throughout the first two decades of the twenty-first century following the almost endless displays of "shoot to kill" orders that seemingly have been given to police officers throughout the country, apparently in order to (permanently) pacify (primarily) African American males.

Again, socialism, in principle, sees African American opportunity as an economic issue at its core—with racism serving as the main weapon upon which the capitalist class depends to control the situation. First, the captains of industry used race-based animosities to keep the working class divided; then, up to and including the modern day, leaders of the capitalist political parties have used race to further fragment the solidarity of workers. Since the Civil War, Democrats and Republicans have usurped major social movements only to declaw them to make them more acceptable to those in power. The radical abolitionist movements were diluted by emancipation, and the freed slaves of 1863 were left to the devices of the Ku Klux Klan and segregationists for at least the next hundred years. The Democratic Party's New Deal of the 1930s consumed the radical wing of economic reform, and over the next fifty years, baptized in the form of government handouts, several generations became dependent, like drug addicts, on economic fixes from the federal supplier.

In Chicago's history, socialist activity was the most successful among women in the decade prior to World War I. While Illinois became the first state east of the Rocky Mountains to grant voting rights to women (in 1913), the mainstream political parties were far from welcoming them into full enfranchisement. With the opening of the presses in the first decade of the twentieth century, the *Socialist Woman* launched its campaign as a strong voice for female suffrage. In a 1909 column, William E. Walling wrote:

> *As long as the community is deprived of the moral force of one-half of the population, the ruling half will continue to be corrupted and to corrupt the whole community by the partial view of human life and human destiny*

The Women's Economic Council in Chicago, 1938. *Courtesy of the Chicago History Museum.*

that are inevitable to any body of people that represents only one-half of the experience of life.[67]

Education was key to Josephine Conger-Kaneko, and she held herself and fellow socialists responsible for the dissemination (and lack thereof) of the philosophies pertinent to the struggle. After the 1908 Socialist Convention in Chicago, fifty-three female members of the party "declared for special propaganda among women" through Socialist literature aimed specifically at them. Conger-Kaneko reflected that times were changing and remembered that five years earlier, women (in general) in Chicago "hadn't a single notion of Socialism."[68] In the same article, she decried the lack of political education with the party using a common "what if/wishful thinking" scenario:

Seven years ago [1902] *there were millions of small boys fourteen years old who, if properly educated would have voted the Socialist ticket last November* [1908, when those boys would have been twenty-one years old]….*Last November* [these youngsters] *voted for Judge Taft* [William Howard Taft].[69]

By this time, the party had increased in membership as well as in activity for women. The Twenty-First Ward branch of the Socialist Party held a meeting on the suffrage issue at the Garrick Theater in the week following Taft's inauguration. Conger-Kaneko covered it and named Chicagoans Gertrude Breslau Hunt, Nellie Zebh, Mary A. Livingston and Corrine Brown as the main speakers.[70] In addition to the recruitment of older women, Conger-Kaneko advocated for the Intercollegiate Socialist Society (ISS) in support of students, particularly female collegians, "copying the revolutionary movements in Germany, Italy and Russia [that were] carried on chiefly by university students." The task of the ISS was to "point out to the hundreds and thousands of poor struggling students…the reasons of the present social conditions and their cure."[71]

The midterm election of 1914 brought many women to the polls. The *Chicago Tribune* recorded 164,026 female voters in the city. Of these, 11,906 voted the Socialist ticket. The paper also credited the female vote for the result of sixteen counties in Illinois "going dry" (banning the sale of alcohol), raising the total number of dry counties in the state to more than thirty. In a celebratory fashion, the *Tribune* identified Alice Collier, of 2542 Artesian Avenue in the Twenty-Eighth Ward, as the first woman to vote in Chicago.[72]

The *Coming Nation*, the third incarnation of Conger-Kaneko's publishing concerns, held up this first salvo from "the weaker sex" as a major blow against sexism and, most importantly, toward the dismantling of the capitalist power structure. In the months prior to the April 1914 municipal election, 217,614 women had registered to vote in Chicago.[73] The accepted final tally showed that well over three-quarters of those who registered actually voted. Out of the city's thirty-five wards, the Twenty-Fifth Ward (including Lincoln Park, Lakeview, Uptown, Edgewater and Rogers Park) had registered the most women, with 10,246 on the rolls.[74] The *Coming Nation* proclaimed limited victory in these numbers as well as in the fact that nine candidates "belonging to the corrupt element" (that is, the Democratic or Republican Party) were defeated, and thirty-three women had been elected to local offices across Illinois.[75]

Eight women put themselves up for seats in the city council in that election. Of the political parties that had women candidates, there was one independent candidate, three from the Progressive Party and four Socialists (Conger-Kaneko, Lida E. McDermut, Mrs. G.R. Dubin and Maude J. Ball);

neither the Democrats nor the Republicans ran a single female candidate.[76] In fact, in the crony-infested First Ward, "Bathhouse John" Coughlin, the notorious political boss and feaster on the city's pre-Capone underbelly, was witnessed by a *Tribune* reporter as he showed his not-so-secret disdain for the issue of suffrage. "The women serving as voter judges and clerks claimed no 'political foresight' by [Coughlin] not distributing candy to the women workers…[but] in one precinct, he handed out cigars to four men on the board there." He was later heard sarcastically ordering a female clerk to light the men's cigars—she did not.[77]

The Socialist candidates ran on a platform of "principles over personal interests, an increase in the number and quality of public schools, wholesome recreation for young people, improved sanitary conditions, rigid inspection of milk and other food, city markets and cheaper coal." Conger-Kaneko pledged that if elected, they "would make it rather hot for the Hinky Dinks (Michael Kenna) and Bathhouse Johns in Chicago's City Council."[78]

While Chicagoans of a socialist bent reveled in the hope of further strength from the new voter bloc, women's suffrage on a national scale would have to wait for seven more years, until the Nineteenth Amendment became official federal law. At the time of the 1914 elections in Illinois, the Democratic-controlled U.S. House of Representatives refused to support women's suffrage on the federal level, claiming that it should be left to the states, as it was not a federal matter.[79] Again, it was the true left wing of the political spectrum that accomplished reform first—or, at least, it moved society further faster than if kept in the hands of those who benefit from maintaining the status quo.

Sadly, it has become the goal of today's Democratic and Republican Parties to promote themselves as being "the party of" women, African Americans, immigrants and marriage equality, among other things. Once again, social movements like women's suffrage, race-based civil rights, immigrant rights and gay rights are being usurped by the ruling class. The ones who fought so strenuously, with so many concrete examples of enfranchisement of these once-excluded groups, are yet again relegated to becoming footnotes in a movement.

The specter of this age-old usurpation is also reappearing in the LGBTQ+ (lesbian, gay, bisexual, transgender, queer and others) communities. In Chicago, these once-ostracized individuals, victims of bigotry and violence, are being used by political and economic manipulators. Regardless of a person's personal beliefs or preferences, the fact is that this culture has shifted in terms of acceptable social norms—and it hasn't been an easy move. After enduring centuries of secrecy, shame and violence, LGBTQ communities are now part of the mainstream. The fifty years after the 1969 Stonewall riots in New York City have shown that even one of the most vilified groups of people can succumb to the curse of normalcy. Pride parades, once the center of courageous vocal protests against stigmatization and bigotry, have accepted corporate sponsorship and the political blessings of lawmakers who suddenly find it expedient to ride in a convertible on the parade route to show their inclusivity—an inclusivity that most kept quiet (or did not display at all) until the 1996 Defense of Marriage Act was declared unconstitutional in 2013.

The less famous who carved their marks on the cornerstones of Chicago are still left in the shadows of the skyscrapers of the infamous residents of this city and nation. The ones who played the game—and still play it today—will be lifted up as models of the competence of their particular group. These manipulators of the historical record have accepted the rules of the political game here in the Windy City just as the founding and current city fathers and mothers do through their incessant blowing of hot air to keep the working class dependent on their patronage and themselves with scepters firmly wedged in their hands. The difference is that today, the wind is blown by representatives from many of the groups that had previously been excluded—they have become part of what earlier men and women had fought against in Chicago, embodying the final words of George Orwell's *Animal Farm*: "Twelve voices were shouting in anger, and they were all alike. No question, now, what had happened to the faces of the pigs. The creatures outside looked from pig to man, and from man to pig, and from pig to man again; but already it was impossible to say which was which."

Chapter 6

THE VOICES AND MUFFLED EARS: A RESTLESS NATION BUILDS AN EMPIRE WITH MONEY TO BURN

The Money Trust [through the consolidation of all larger banks by the
Federal Reserve Board] *would be able to make money scarce or
plentiful as it pleases.*[80]
—*Burke McCarty in the* Coming Nation, *1913*

T he dawning of the twentieth century marked the beginnings of an
awareness throughout the United States of a maturing nation on
the world stage. It had been born in a daring feat of rebellion against the
imperial power of England and had grown to become, within 125 years of
independence, an imperial power that rivaled those of Europe. Socialists
condemned the war against Spain in 1898 as a territory-grabbing maneuver
that sought only the material benefit of a U.S. brand of colonialism. It was
slavery that chained the indigenous peoples in the Caribbean and Pacific
island holdings of the dying Spanish Empire to lifelong servitude at fruit
and sugar companies. In 1903, with the passage of the Efficiency of Militia
Act, all able-bodied men in the United States between eighteen and forty-
five years old became potential conscripts into the militia at the president's
call—an ample supply of muscle for the young empire.[81]

This was seen at the time (and into our own time) as governmental action
in favor of U.S. corporate interests throughout the territorial holdings of the
United States as well as those in other countries where "American interests"
were threatened. One can interpret the phrase "American interests" and see
through it the socialistic basis for protest against interventionist policies in the

Middle East. This is most keenly witnessed in Iraq and Afghanistan, where oil flows and poppies grow to feed the insatiable appetite for automobile transportation and drugs, respectively.

Domestically, in the aftermath of the U.S. victory over a gasping Spain, socialist labor leaders, politicians and journalists in Chicago kept pressure on employers as well as whole industries to improve living conditions in the city. Probably the most famous author from this period, Upton Sinclair, was, in 1904, just finishing his undercover work in the stockyards on the south side of town. *The Jungle* chronicled the life of immigrant workers in the meatpacking industry and exposed the foul practices and conditions of those condemned to scrape out a living among the scrapings of animal carcasses. This piece of socialistic journalism served to guide the hand of social reform as Democrats and Republicans energetically joined in to demand greater oversight of the food industry—well after others had been demanding this for years.

Working conditions and wages were not the only issues addressed by Socialists. The prices of essentials rose and fell according to availability and need—in a system in which those who can afford more make most of the rules, the law of supply and demand dictated that wages of the working class were seldom adequate for them to enjoy a self-sufficient, comfortable life like the lives of those for whom they toiled. The powerless will constantly seek ways to exert power over those who wield more of it. In order to effect change, there were calls for not just strikes but also for boycotts of the products used and needed every day. In 1913, Josephine Conger-Kaneko, in the *Coming Nation*, called for all purchases of eggs in New York, Cleveland and Chicago to stop for three to six weeks as a protest against high prices. She advocated for the establishment of municipal chicken farms so that eggs could be obtained at cost and thereby made affordable to all.[82]

In 1909, the *Coming Nation* came out as a strong opposing voice to the Payne-Aldrich Tariff Act that was passed in April of that year. Although it was viewed as compromise legislation between the two ruling parties, Conger-Kaneko condemned the new law as another attack against the working class. It set about fixing duties (import taxes) on household goods, most of which were seen as necessities—of course, the added cost would be absorbed by the consumer. The tariff, then, is money paid by the consumer over and above the cost of producing an item in order to protect the manufacturer against cheap items being imported from overseas.[83] In our own day, tariffs have been used by governments as economic tools in the game of world trade; the reality is that more often than not, the tariff is used as a weapon in the ongoing battle against the lower classes in all countries. Nations play these economic games as if on a board, with their own citizens serving as pieces to be manipulated as necessary.

As quoted at the beginning of this chapter, Burke McCarty, along with Conger-Kaneko, saw the consolidation of wealth in the hands of a few as a threat to the majority of people. The Money Trust—those organizations that control wealth (banks, industrial magnates, governments and speculators)—would, he claimed, "own the railroads, the mines, forests, fisheries, public utilities and big industries, and they are very much interested in the stock market, and will gratefully accept an arrangement by which they can make money plentiful or scarce, and [create] a bull or bear market."[84] Thomas Morgan, a ubiquitous Chicago Socialist since 1873, added his voice to the warning against the new flexing of economic muscle by the few as early as the 1890s by boldly presenting "A Socialist's View of the Trusts" at a Chicago conference on trusts.[85] However, it would be the "trustbusters" of a different species (Theodore Roosevelt and others) who would win credit for taming the beast of unbridled capitalism.

The historical record has shown that it is a disenfranchised left that has consistently raised the banner of real social change in this country, while

"Carrying the Message" in Chicago, April 1992. *Courtesy of the Chicago History Museum* (CHM: i023702_pm).

the accepted ruling political parties—currently Democrats and Republicans (both of which are neoliberal at best and conservative at worst in terms of the larger political spectrum)—have supported revolutionary ideas only after the movements have been brought to heel. The regular filibustering against solid social reform by conservatives is consistent (most Democrats are merely the liberal wing of the conservative party, as they wish, along with Republicans, to keep the system as it is). The worn-out sanctimony of Republicans and annoying self-righteousness of Democrats have crippled progress in the areas of labor reform, eradication of poverty, educational reform, real health-care reform and a massive reduction in "defense spending" (a euphemism for the building and maintenance of an empire).

But since the middle of the nineteenth century, it has been the people who have handed power to the two ruling parties. The presidential election of 1856 was when Democrats and Republicans went head to head for the first time, and although the path has been long and winding, the narrowing of political options in the United States to just two parties has allowed the vultures of today to feast on the carcass of the republic. It is with few exceptions that a viable third party has risen to challenge the political status quo in any real sense over the past century and a half. News anchors and pundits prattle on about "red and blue" states; the major networks and social media outlets give prime attention to the candidates from the two capitalistic parties; state legislatures continue to legally conspire, because they make the laws, to keep third parties off state ballots as often as possible. The signature requirements in the state of Illinois and Chicago are thinly veiled attempts to keep non-machine candidates off the ballots, as signatures benefit those with name recognition or overstuffed war chests of cash; these requirements hardly help fresh faces make their way to the stage or new blood to flow into the system.

That system is funded by business interests that have benefited from political backroom handshakes and winks and from planting themselves on the seats of government influence and favor. Chicago—the notorious "City on the Make," "most violent city," "Seat of Organized Crime and Organized Labor" and "City of Big Shoulders"—and its people must come to terms with the city's past and present in order to alter its course for the future.

Chapter 7

SCHOOL DAZE: DAZZLING STATISTICS AND CORRECTING HISTORY

Would they [teachers' unions] *continue to opt for an insider strategy, praising the neo-liberal politicians and titans of capital who wanted to destroy them, in the hopes that perhaps, if they were sufficiently deferential, these forces would spare them and their members? Or would they confront those enemies head on, with militant tactics like strikes and deep organizing within communities?* [86]
—*Micah Uetricht on the 2012 Chicago teachers' strike*

Wealth and poverty have been human realities as long as there have been differences in ability and opportunity. The relationship between wealth, poverty and education has long been debated. Historically, in Chicago, this argument has been led by reformers of all types; this section will focus on those of the socialistic stripe. As previously stated, one of the official Socialist Party's founding planks in its 1876 platform for change was regarding the abolition of child labor and the adoption of universal education. These two issues are closely linked to higher wages for adults; more just pay for them means that their children do not need to provide income for the family and can therefore attend school. In addition to the benefit of higher wages, this increases the possibility of access to healthier food and more sanitary conditions at home and in the workplace.

It is important to note that it was not until 1938, upon the passage of the Fair Labor Standards Act (FLSA), that federal law, applicable in all states, banned "oppressive child labor." Prior to this, the recognized accepted work age (the age of a "wage earner," as defined by the U.S. Census Bureau until

Chicagoans waiting for work permits. *Courtesy of the Chicago History Museum.*

1940) was ten years old and older.[87] After the passage of the FLSA, a wage earner was defined as being fourteen years old and older. Today, the youngest age at which a worker may be employed as a defined wage earner is sixteen, with restrictions of hours and time of day in a given job while in high school.

One of the accepted keys to a solid future is literacy. At the start of the twentieth century, evidence seems to point to an incremental improvement in Chicago, with some understandable spikes in illiteracy due to immigration. The definition of literacy has changed over time: at the end of the nineteenth century, being considered "literate" meant that one was able to read and write in English, or able to do one of the two. By 1890, generational differences were already noticeable in the census records. The generation born around the time of the Civil War and up to the 1877 national strikes and who reached the ages of twenty to thirty-five in the last decade of the nineteenth century while being unable to read or write was about 15,000 citizens. Those who were illiterate in the ten- to nineteen-year-old category totaled about 3,200.[88]

The total Chicago population who were ten years old and older and were illiterate in 1890 included, as broken down by the federal government according to race and citizenship: "Negros," 1,657 (12.5 percent of that group); "Foreign Born White," 35,704 (8.3 percent of that group); and "Native Born White," 1,685 (.4 percent of that group).[89] By 1920, while the total populations in Chicago in all three groups had significantly increased, the illiteracy rates increased, too. This is understandable and can be attributed to the waves of poorer, uneducated, rural Europeans and African Americans who migrated from the southern states into the city. (The author, being a very proud descendant of poor southern Italians and Sicilians, is aware of the pejorative tone of the adjectives but begs the reader's tolerance.)

The number of African Americans in Chicago who were illiterate in any language (the government's definition of literacy was changed in 1908) rose to nearly 3,800, but because of the increase in population due to the "Great Migration" from the former Confederacy, the overall illiteracy rate of this group in the city dropped to 3.9 percent by 1920 (down from the 12.5 percent of thirty years prior). This represented the largest increase in the ability to read and write of the three population groups. The immigrant group unable to read or write in any language increased to 92,473 (11.6 percent). The native-born white population in the city unable to read or write increased slightly to 2,419 (with the overall rate dropping to .2 percent).[90]

In spite of the improvements made in basic literacy, solid educational reform was elusive in Chicago. By 1920, the census breakdown of regular school attendance reveals a significant drop of at least 40 percent of the student population over the age of fourteen; this is across the board, as it were, and includes all students regardless of gender and/or racial or ethnic identity; almost half of all Chicago adolescents were not attending high school so that they could work full-time.[91] A pattern can be traced using Chicago Public School statistics: garnering the records from three academic years over a generation, one can see a large disparity between school enrollment and actual average daily attendance. In 1881, the rolls show 63,141 students (between ten and eighteen years old), with 44,200 of them showing up every day. In 1891, out of 146,751 registered students, 108,137 were daily attenders. In 1901, the 262,738 students had an attendance number of 208,081.[92] By 1910, the census records show that the percentage of students in this age group who dropped out of school—again, regardless of gender or race—grew to between 60 and 70 percent.[93]

Ensuring students' full-time attendance is a challenge for every school district at all times. Today, graduation rates are seen as one way to measure the strength of an educational system. Chicago has seen a large increase in the first two decades of the twenty-first century: in the 2017–18 school year,

The Chicago Hammond School, 1895. *Courtesy of the Chicago History Museum.*

78.2 percent of the city's public-school students graduated. While this still leaves roughly one in four students not graduating high school, it is a major improvement from the 56.9 percent of the 2010–11 academic year.[94]

The improvements in school attendance after World War I occurred among the youngest students (ages seven to thirteen). By 1920, the city saw over 90 percent of this population attending school, while the rate of their employment, at least part-time, dropped to less than 1 percent.[95] By 1940, child labor became a nonissue in this age group due to the federal mandate prohibiting those under fourteen from working.

While the battle against "oppressive child labor" is over in the United States, the struggle for quality educational reform continues in all school districts. In Illinois, conflicts continue over equitable funding within the entire state as well as in Chicago, specifically. The outmoded use of property tax codes as the basis for allocation of money to schools satisfies few—with the exception, perhaps, of legislators and city council members who benefit by having expertise in property tax law.

In Chicago, one of the most controversial issues regarding funding of any kind is related to Tax Increment Financing (the notorious "TIF money").

Under Mayors Richard Daley (the second) and Rahm Emanuel, this money (its use restricted by Illinois law) is collected as a fund for each TIF district set up by the city; upon being set up as a TIF district, the average amount of tax money collected (Equalized Assessed Valuation, or EAV) each year over a period of twenty-three years of the district having been established is set as the base. After property taxes are collected from that specific area, the amount over that EAV calculation is kept in the district for use in development.[96] All is well and good—in theory. The problem, as always, comes in the practice. At the end of Mayor Rahm Emanuel's first term in 2015, there was $1.3 billion in TIF funds throughout the city's seven TIF districts, with 48 percent of the total overflowing in the coffers of the "Central District" of downtown—the Loop and Gold Coast business district. The "South District" received 16 percent, the "Northwest" received 10 percent, both "North" and "West" received 9 percent and the "Far South" and "Southwest" sections received a paltry 4 percent each.[97] The justification for the imbalance between the districts is that the revenue given back in the business districts will eventually help the entire city.

This is an example of the theory of "trickle-down economics" that was made famous in the 1980s with President Ronald Reagan as its most vocal proponent. The belief is a tired relic of capitalist justification theory—that if the government grants concessions, tax incentives and outright gifts of money to big business, this, in turn, will spur industry to reinvest in their companies, which will, according to the economic theory, bring prosperity to the whole, including the working class—"from the top down."

A metaphor can help here: imagine a pyramid of stacked wine glasses: a large bottle of wine is poured into the top glass, and the overflowing wine trickles down into the other glasses until all are filled. Again, theories are flawless! The problem comes in the implementation of any theory in the existing order; the wine might be poured into the top glass, but that top glass is continually being swapped out for a larger glass, and the lower glasses remain empty, or a few might get a splashing, at best, of the bounty from the top. The pyramid is stacked by a set group of people, their political lackies, their descendants and a few others who benefit from the game being played with the rules kept intact. This has been socialism's claim since the beginning—that too few are in control of too much.

Even in the twenty-first century, although we have landed robots on Mars, the City of Chicago and State of Illinois cannot get out of the antiquated materialism of political chicanery to benefit lawmakers who have embedded themselves with business. The laws governing the establishment of the TIF districts and the collection and distribution of funds are all controlled by the same self-serving hydras that citizens continue to elect and reelect. School districts will continue to have to beg for funding, teachers will continue to spend their own money to supply their classrooms and the students will continue to suffer—apparently, this is acceptable in order to keep things as they are, to keep the lid atop the boiling water.

There are safeguards that exist in any system to keep that system intact, be it through walls, moats, armor, legislation or inaction. Public education in Chicago is the product of such a siege mentality. Real educational reform—actual change that benefits students—is hampered by the typical good-old-boyism that has infected the political bloodstream as open sewage once polluted the Chicago River. The city's school system is one of very few in the United States that has an appointed board of education (appointed by the mayor), as codified in state law since 1995. The board is accountable to the mayor alone—not the public.

The same "quarterback sneak" is going on among the charter schools in the city. Long seen as the financial salvation of public education, these schools, funded by independent corporate money, hand off accountability from the public to private sponsors—taxpayers have little voice in this system. The citizens can't seem to find "the ball" of educational accountability because it has been secretly passed from unelected official to private sponsors. When business interests dictate educational policy, the danger of the atrophy of students' critical and creative thinking abilities will be assured. Industrialists, bankers and land barons will guarantee themselves an obedient, unthinking generation of workers. Those in control will continue to cheer themselves by mandating, relying on and baiting educators with standardized testing.

What was told to this author over thirty years ago in education classes at St. Mary's College (where teachers would never have to "teach to the test") has come to pass. Legislators with legal and financial training—but little or no educational expertise, and with the special interests of business leaders and faux educators in the standardized testing industry (a multibillion-dollar enterprise) in mind—dictate educational policy and performance expectations to educators, parents (the first teachers of their own children) and students themselves. This is accepted by the public because of an insatiable need to trust the very people who are the manipulators. The public finds it difficult to conceive of anything except that which it is fed by the power brokers and pimps who pull the strings behind that power.

We accept quick solutions because we lack the will to struggle with perplexing problems such as funding for education. Gambling, once the

Chicago Teachers Union demonstration, 1930s. *Courtesy of the Chicago History Museum.*

bastion of organized crime, has become the acceptable drug of choice for most state legislators and local government officials by offering the fictitious promise of an unending stream of capital pouring into the coffers of state treasuries and city halls. And what is the miracle source of this income? It is the poor and working classes—the wealthy don't need to buy lottery tickets. Among those who are assured of bonuses, fat paychecks and dividend profits, there is no need to gamble for a financial windfall; the wealthy do not often find themselves in the parking lots of convenience stores littered with scratch-off stubs, the discarded hopes of those on whom the lies of government swindlers have fallen.

And what has happened to the budgetary savior? Where has all this lottery money gone? The percentage that a winning individual receives can be witnessed on the news. But what of the tax revenue for city, state and federal governments? Somebody's pockets are being lined (and it's not those of the teachers); and city streets are certainly not lined with gold—ask anyone driving over potholes.

Military spending far exceeds any outlay given by the federal government at this time—in 2017 alone, 54 percent of the annual budget, according to the Office of Management and Budget, was devoted to "defense spending." One can say what one will with respect to a need for a strong military, but the reality is that the United States bears part of the responsibility for the hypermilitarism of our world—others are equally responsible, but if the United States' position as world leader is to be upheld, there must be a way to begin the restoration of sanity and charity on the political stage without saber-rattling and wall-building.

We see an inability to think and problem-solve as the norm in the "Baby Boom" generation of leadership. That population grew up in the post–World War II era of pragmatism and "hard work," with creativity a far-off fuzziness better left to radicals and beatniks. The "Greatest Generation," to borrow Tom Brokaw's phrase, lived through the Great Depression and defeated the Nazis and Imperial Japan; Americans were capable of anything. This attitude led the nation into the swamps of war in Korea and Southeast Asia. The hardheadedness of the administrations of Truman, Eisenhower, Kennedy, Johnson and Nixon allowed for the atomic and conventional destruction of hundreds of thousands of human beings at a time when Communist leaders in the Soviet Union, Cuba, Cambodia and China were doing the same thing. And around the world, poverty—physical and moral—increased. The building of empires under the "Stars and Stripes" or the "Hammer and Sickle" has meant that the working class, the poor and the migrant will always pay a higher price for their leaders' petty but deadly games on the world chessboard, and the game continues to be a barrier to real social progress.

One need not look across the globe and down the timeline of history to see this pattern. In state capitals throughout the country and in Washington, D.C., incompetent politicians are handed the reins of power by ignorant voters. These politicians (the era of statesmen is long dead) only turn up the heat on vitriol and hate-speak, stifling real debate and the search for real solutions to any social problem. At the present time, there is no viable alternative to the two ruling capitalist parties; they will continue to snipe at each other until the day when the electorate wrenches political power from their lecherous fists and attains social liberation.

Chapter 8

BUSINESS IS BUSINESS, BUT WHOSE BUSINESS IS IT?: LOSING SIGHT AND LOSING THE BATTLE

I have commanded my soul to be silent,
This tin-can Chicago must not be tied to me,
These women hanging their talons on me, fastening their hungry lips on me,
And these men, red with the slaughter of ten million dreams—red from the blood
of hogs and women…
These are the tin-cans of the world, they must not be tied to me…
I have commanded my soul to silence and to scorn.[98]
—Loureine Aber

Lest one think this work is a diatribe against business and profit, one need only remember that the goal of a workable socialism, as argued for in these pages, centers on equity and the realization that society will only grow and continue to exist if all of its members see their common bond. Politicians and leaders of business have got to be brought to heel and under control of the people who elect them, provide labor and keep the shops open with their purchasing power. Anyone in a position of power should be accountable to those who vote or buy things as well as those who don't vote or who boycott a business.

Even socialists, sadly, have seen the necessity of this "pandering" to a particular base. The pages of Josephine Conger-Kaneko's journals were peppered with advertisements for all sorts of products—some of them blatant scams and cheap pleas involving moneymaking schemes. The *Progressive Woman*, the *Socialist Woman* and the *Coming Nation* were not immune from the murky world of commercialism and included ads for things that ranged from children's clothes to food and furniture to fortune tellers and beauty treatments. Illinois women may have won the right to vote in 1913, seven years before the Nineteenth Amendment went into effect, but businessmen knew how to manipulate, and the journals of the left accepted some social conventions.

In one advertisement, the inventers of a skin cream called Browntone boasted that it was the "greatest foe to Old Age—the surest aid to attractiveness," because it was "every woman's duty to keep young."[99] The *Coming Nation* peppered its pages with the promise for the "bust developed rapidly, one ounce a day," and the reason given was that "no woman should neglect an opportunity to escape the pain and heartache of being skinny, scrawny, angular and unattractive in body."[100] Men were not immune to the social pressure of a preordained vision of beauty; in one of the last issues of the journal, just before the outbreak of World War I in Europe, an ad for gaining "22 pounds in 23 days" foretold that "you" could "quickly put from ten to thirty pounds of good, solid, 'stay there' flesh, fat and muscular tissue between your skin and bones."[101] Even get-rich-quick schemes were a real temptation for non-materialistic leftists: "Gold in Mexico?" was being "ground out, and when the big fellows learn of this the opportunity to get in will be gone forever."[102] The *Coming Nation* didn't seem to be concerned about the social ramifications of speculation, mining in other peoples' backyards or the probable use of slave labor to extract the minerals from the ground. This serves as an example of how all people are susceptible to losing focus on basic principles if a consistent rational thought process is not followed.

Advertisements in a socialist journal are a small matter compared with the assault that has been launched against socialism because of the totalitarian practices of some self-proclaimed "communist" governments, namely the Soviet Union, China, Cambodia, North Korea and Cuba. These were all promised worker utopias that quickly turned into oligarchic dictatorships of terror for the average citizen and much material gain for the few in power. They have never deserved refuge under the umbrella of socialism in any sense of the word except for the fact that they usurped the philosophy, quickly discarded it and abandoned the proletariat they had pledged to uplift.

A more just socialism will strive to benefit every member of a society by trying to coax the wealthy to assist those less fortunate with lifting themselves up while still seeking a more equitable distribution of material goods. The tired old clichés of Marxist class struggle have got to be abandoned along with the skewed assumptions that all business would be

Cover of the prewar issue of the *Coming Nation*, 1914. *Courtesy of the Newberry Library and Nathanael Filbert.*

run by the government in order to establish some robotic society of blind obedience to Big Brother.

In the field of socialistic journalism, the First World War provided much fodder as the carnage of the belligerents piled up on the fields of Flanders and in the Alps, the Middle East, Asia and across Poland and Russia. The main players in the war (Germany, Austria-Hungary, England, France, Russia and Italy) saw economic gain, land-grabbing and the dominance of Europe as casus belli, or justification for war. As was typical of the men in power at that time, they were most energetic when it came to committing the lives of the younger generation to slaughter. As they fumbled into war along with the countless men and women who were oblivious to the cost of their leaders' toxic masculinity, greed, lust for power and nationalism were used to breed insidious propaganda up to that time, hurling half the globe into war.[103]

Socialists throughout the world voiced a consistent but unconnected opposition to the war. In Chicago, as the conservative Democratic and Republican Parties joined the rising chorus to support England and France against Germany (referred to in wartime propaganda as "the Huns"), those who protested such jingoism were monitored, censored and imprisoned. Although the United States didn't enter the war until April 6, 1917, official U.S. diplomatic support of the Allies was clear from the beginning of the conflict.

As the fighting dragged on in Europe, among the American people, support of the war grew, too. In Chicago, which had a large German population and Socialist organizations heavily populated with Germans, both groups were suspect. With the passage of the Espionage Act on June 15, 1917, and the "blowing the dust off" of the Alien and Sedition Acts of 1798, the federal government easily silenced opposition leadership. Eugene Debs, a national figure of the Socialist movement since the Pullman Strike of 1894, was arrested in 1918 and charged with violating the Espionage and Sedition Acts during his vocal protests against the war and U.S. involvement in it; he was convicted and eventually went to prison in 1919. He ran for president as a Socialist candidate for his fifth and final time in 1920, becoming the first candidate in U.S. history to run for president while in prison.

Chicagoans suffered similar persecution and prosecution at the hands of city and federal officials. In the days of war on foreign soil, the U.S. Postal Censor's office was very active in terms of suspicion of U.S. citizens. In letters to Chicago city attorney P.J. Barry, the 1918 case of Mary Marcy was explained by an unidentified federal official. "Regarding the parcel…you are advised that as the pamphlet…has been declared to be non-mailable under the Espionage Act, the parcel will be retained in the files of this office."[104] Early the next year, Edward Bell, of the U.S. Embassy in London, wrote to his superiors in Washington, D.C.:

> *You will observe from this [enclosed] letter* [dated 11 January 1919: Mary Marcy and Esa Unterman to Ben Tillett in London] *that the woman Marcy is an IWW* [i.e. a member of the Industrial Workers of the World] *and describes the recent leaders of the AFL* [American Federation of Labor] *as reactionary; also that she is anxious to get* [Eugene] *Debs and* [William "Big Bill"] *Haywood out of jail. In view of this woman's associates it might be as well to keep her under observation if this has not already been done.*[105]

In this same communique, Bell went on to name others in Chicago and London whose letters had been confiscated: Robert Blatchford, Robert Smillie and Silvia Pankhurst.[106]

Now, it is important to remember for the sake of understanding the fuller picture (but not to excuse xenophobia and censorship) that the tone in the United States at this time was hypersensitive. The passenger ship *Lusitania* had been sunk by German submarines in 1915, and in the spring of 1917, the infamous "Zimmerman Telegram" was intercepted and decoded by the British. The telegram exposed a German attempt to form an alliance with Mexico against the Allies; in exchange, Germany promised Mexico that if the United States entered the war as an ally of England, France and other Allied countries, Germany would see to the return to Mexico of most of the territories seized by the United States in the Mexican-American War—namely Texas, Arizona and New Mexico. While the Germans never denied the contents of the telegram, Americans saw this attempt as the clear intention of the Central Powers ("the enemy") to destroy civilization, including the inviolable borders we had so righteously attained.

The telegram was less nefarious than the U.S. propaganda machine claimed: Germany was doing nothing more than was traditional at the time in terms of wooing potential associates to their cause. England and France had lured Italy to the Allied side in 1915 by promising the less successful but most imperial descendants of the Romans more territorial gains than Germany and Austria-Hungary had promised them. Though national boundaries are movable, as history teaches, most Americans have swallowed the doctrine of Manifest Destiny—the belief that it has been ordained and established that the United States would stretch from sea to shining sea; it's in a song, therefore it must be true.

Fear of domestic intrigue aside, the atmosphere for Socialists in Chicago during and immediately after World War I was toxic. Faced with censure, imprisonment and ostracism, the left was weakened, and a type of diaspora began. Many, like William Haywood, fled to the Bolsheviks of Russia; others remained in prison until their confinement expired or they, like Eugene Debs, received a presidential pardon. With the success of the persecution of protestors, the growing exposure of the early Soviet Union as a less-than-utopian workers' paradise (especially as Joseph Stalin tightened his imperialistic grip on the people who so recently had been strangled by the czars), and the resurrection of the age-old capitalist fear of anything approaching any type of communism, socialism went into a dormancy and wouldn't awaken and find its voice again until well after the McCarthy era of the 1950s.

In the twenty-first century, as leadership did during the First World War, the two ruling parties conspired to manipulate popular fears after the attacks of September 11, 2001. The Patriot Act passed quickly and overwhelmingly in the wake of the first attacks against civilians on U.S. soil since the burning of the White House by the British during the War of 1812 (Pearl Harbor, being a military attack, is in a different category). The Patriot Act garnered much protest from a growing and popular left wing, but the law was enacted after it passed in both houses of Congress with a vote of 357–66 (with 6 members not voting) in the House and 98–1 (with 1 not voting) in the Senate.[107] The Patriot Act survived through the administrations of George W. Bush and Barack Obama, morphing into the Freedom Act of 2015, and, as of summer 2019, lives on during the Trump presidency.

A healthy democracy will only exist if protest and alternative voices are allowed to flourish. Fear never breeds reasoned response. Inquisitions, expulsions of whole populations, enemy lists, usurpation and the manipulation of the rule of law will all end with—at best—a people's rejection of doctrine or—at worst—violent upheaval.

Chapter 9

WHERE HAVE ALL THE CHILDREN GONE?: SOCIALISM, MORE WAR AND CORPORATE VIOLENCE

The government will never protect [the people] *unless the citizens operate to make sure the government protects them.*[108]
—*Ralph Nader*

With the rise of the Soviet Union from the 1920s onward, socialism became identified with communism, and, after the signing of the 1939 German-Soviet Non-Aggression Pact, with the totalitarianism of both Joseph Stalin and Adolf Hitler. In Chicago, the Socialist Party limped into the municipal elections of 1923, with William Cunnea garnering 41,186 votes; the Republican, Arthur C. Leuder, got 285,094 votes, and the victor, Democrat William Emmett Dever, received 390,413 votes. It was to be the last time the Socialist Party would have a candidate in Chicago's mayoral elections until Willie Mae Reid in 1975.

The American political system, news outlets, movie industry and the public itself all saw socialism in the Soviet style. With the added sinister elements of what seemed to be a mob-infested labor movement, an active spy network (confirmed by the convictions of Ethel and Julius Rosenberg), the possession of atomic weapons by the Soviet Union and China (for some reason, it was assumed that the United States should be the sole caretakers of atomic weapons) and the far-flung militaristic philosophy of political fossils with trigger fingers that claimed the world was "going red," the United States had to lead the fight against it. As during the run-up to World War I, criticism of U.S. policy equaled treason. The ruling parties succeeded

Edward J. Kelly (*left*) and Patrick A. Nash, of the infamous Kelly-Nash Machine that reigned over Chicago from 1933 to 1943. *Courtesy of the Chicago History Museum.*

in squelching alternative views, and the world was kept in a state of terror, stupefied by the doctrine of mutually assured destruction (both the communist and "free" worlds had the nuclear capability to destroy the other); it's not a coincidence that the acronym for this doctrine is "MAD."

On the local level, Chicago mimicked the game on the worldwide chessboard. The city would settle into its political comfort zone after Mayor William Dever's reign, with the last gasp of the Republican Party in Chicago's city hall as William Hale Thompson took the throne in 1927. The Democrats would wrench control of the council and the mayor's office with Anton Cermak's victory in 1931 and hold onto power through the second decade of the twenty-first century. After Cermak's assassination in 1933 and a six-month transition to Mayor Frank Corr, Edward J. Kelly (the lapdog of Patrick A. Nash) manipulated the workings of the city in what has been called "the Kelly-Nash Machine" until 1947. Martin H. Kennelly guided the crooked flow of the city until 1955 and was followed by Richard J. Daley, whose rule ended with his death in 1976.[109]

In the 1960s, the left and "outsiders" from everywhere were blamed for every rumple of the political fabric in Chicago. Martin Luther King met with violent protests, abuse and obstruction in his time in the city during the summer of 1966. The now-iconic brutal repression of protestors while "the whole world was watching" during the 1968 Democratic National Convention and the killings of Fred Hampton and Mark Clark on December 4, 1969, gave the (Richard J.) Daley Administration its reputation of staunch inflexibility in the face of opposition of any kind. Copying the Johnson Administration in the White House and the Agitator Index of the Federal Bureau of Investigation, Daley's Red Squad helped keep opposition groups in the realm of suspicion, guaranteeing such "extremists" had no room at the table in Chicago politics.

In the aftermath of the protests and assassinations of 1968, the 1969 and 1970 bombings of the Police Memorial (near the site of the Haymarket Riot) by the Students for a Democratic Society (also known as the Weathermen), socialism seemed to have recovered part of its voice. Willie Mae Reid, of the Socialist Workers Party, ran for mayor in 1975 and received 16,749 votes; this was only 2 percent of the total, but—along with the other party members running for city clerk (Antonio DeLeon) and treasurer (Nancy Rosenstock)—it represented the return of socialism to the political sphere in the city.[110] Mayor Richard J. Daley locked in his sixth term with 78 percent of the vote.[111]

Willie Mae Reid, Socialist Workers Party candidate for mayor of Chicago in 1975. *Courtesy of Mark PoKempner for* Chicago Reader.

Reid was outspoken on the issue of police spying in Chicago. In the wake of investigations, she said, "When the disclosures first came out…Daley said it didn't happen; then he changed his story to say spying was necessary to stop groups from being violent."[112] As has so often happened, fear was used to justify breaches in constitutional protections, and it's up to the true reformers and radicals to bring such shady activity into the light.

During the mid-1970s, the socialist platform contained a push for free public transportation, along with citizen oversight and control, with a tax on merchants and employers whose workers use it. This plank was seen as a method to reduce automobile traffic in the city and boost employment opportunities. The party also supported nursing-home reform and the establishment of community organizations to investigate jails, hospitals and police shootings. It criticized the educational system "designed years ago to turn out folks from some schools to push wheelbarrows and folks from other schools to push people."[113]

At the same time as the broadcast of this call for social realignment, the Black Workers Congress met in 1971 with a growing leftist voice. Activist John Watson spoke about African American labor in the Midwest, saying that "the mighty fortresses of General Motors, IBM, U.S. Steel, etc., are all laid on a foundation of Black and Brown blood, sweat and tears."[114] He accused the conglomerates of manipulating African American and Latino workers, using them as a wedge to force down wages, and freezing the income of the entire working class without any serious attempt at price freezing.[115] At the same conference, Michele Russell presented a paper by Harold Brown expressing the traditional line but in the contemporary field: "We know now that we and the Cubans are fighting the same enemy and that the enemy is the whole system; a brutal international economic and political system of organization and control."[116]

This is the overarching critique of the political/economic system as it has always existed. But theory is never enough to spur an entire people to change anything—the impetus is always a people's reality of housing, educational and employment opportunities, security and cost of living in the day-to-day world. These are the avenues through which people have a satisfactory or unsatisfactory life. These issues are the source of the cry of a people.

Socialists attempted to keep these issues at the fore. In the early 1970s, a sluggish political structure, reeling from the pummeling of the previous decade, attempted to address some of them. After the 1970 U.S. Census, the Department of Housing and Urban Development (HUD) developed the "Model Cities Program," in which Chicago participated. Through the

Demonstration Cities Act of 1967, an outline had been developed to launch "a coordinated attack…to substantially improve the living environment and the general welfare of people living in slum and blighted neighborhoods."[117] However, like the Illinois legislature's committee work in the 1870s and early 1900s, the chatter and paperwork is only useful if the words spoken and written are supported by deeds.

The Model Cities Program was developed by the same government officials (and their politico-corporate predecessors) who oversaw the creation of the interstate highway system, which leveled neighborhoods and paved the way for the great "white flight" from cities to the suburbs— just one cause of the inner-city mess of the last seventy-five years. Political hypocrisy seems to have been reborn with more blather and finger-wagging regarding housing in Chicago, while city council members allow their neighborhoods to become increasingly gentrified (that is to say, "prettied up" so that developers can buy property, displace residents, tear down homes and build multiunit dwellings for astronomical profit). Once again, those who hold the reins of power and influence have jostled their way into profiting with respect to property sales and taxation authority.

These men and women have remained in their seats (of power) because the voters have kept them there, and the saga of Chicago continues to be written by the same group and at the expense of the average citizen. However, the spring 2019 municipal elections seem to indicate change: Chicagoans are raising a slow but hopeful hand to reverse the flow of political privilege. And the working class will continue to work, always with an eye on survival and a distant hope that things will change. It still remains to be seen if this change can be more than the stuff of pipe dreams.

But the disparity continues. A report by Richard Saul Wurman, creator of the TED conferences, titled "Wealth and Poverty 2000" looked at the salaries of both the average worker and the average chief executive officer in the United States in 1997. Near the start of the twenty-first century, a man or woman could expect to earn about $27,000 per year; the average CEO could look forward to an annual salary of just over $4 million.[118] Median income in the nation was about $39,000, and a mere .1 percent of citizens made over $1 million.[119] According to the 2000 U.S. Census, the number of people living in poverty (defined at the time by the U.S. Census Bureau as an income of $17,000 or less for a family of four) in Chicago was 559,859 (19.5 percent of its population, compared to the national rate of 12.7 percent).[120] By 2017, with the poverty line drawn at $25,000 for a family of four, 20.6 percent of Chicagoans had incomes at or below this level.[121]

Poverty will remain a major issue, along with educational reform and economic opportunity, in the nation and Chicago as long as the same leadership continues to connive to remain in power and fail to lead. A successful challenge to the established order has got to come to the fore, building strength from a handful of city council seats, and continue to make itself known if an alternative solution is to be found. There is not a unified voice of opposition at this time, and because of that void, there has been no viable slate of candidates who could face off against the business-as-usual candidates in either Washington or Chicago.

A fragmented socialism still fought and continued to slate candidates into the 1990s while facing the typical crooked rules of electoral practice. In 1975, "minor parties" were required to get 56,000 signatures to be able to be placed on the ballot in Chicago; a candidate of one of the two "major parties" needed only 4,000.[122] Socialist Party candidate John Brisben launched an unsuccessful write-in campaign just a few months before the 1975 mayoral election. Other socialists who ran as mayoral candidates included Dennis Brasky (1977), Andrew Pulley (1979) and James Warren (1991). To date, they have been the last candidates for mayor who publicly ran as socialists in Chicago.

Even though the rules have changed in Illinois and Chicago, with any given candidate required to get 12,000 signatures, the laws that have been written by the members of the two ruling parties favor those in power and with greater name recognition; the candidates must garner more signatures than are actually required in order to have the minimum number after challenges are made to signatures (a noble rule enacted to minimize fraud). But, again, an incumbent is the usual beneficiary over any new names on a candidate list, and incumbents can be counted on, more often than not, to protect business interests.

Ralph Nader, who has been at the forefront of consumer advocacy for over fifty years and is the poster child for the Green Party in the United States, has been a consistent voice for the left in his work for the rights of people to be informed and kept safe in an atmosphere of "corporate violence" against them.[123] Since at least the nineteenth century, the drive for profit has provided the impetus for multibillion-dollar companies to pump chemicals into rivers, oceans and farmland; the same drive for profit has allowed for the production of dangerous items in households and on the roads. This "silent violence" (as opposed to the street violence that is well televised every day) of pollutants in the air and water and soil, fossil fuel–powered vehicles, food additives and readily accessible opiates is allowed to be enacted because of the support of legislators. As early as the 1960s, Nader and others on the grassroots level called on the government to protect citizens against "the pell-mell rush for profits" and the looting of the public.[124] Again, political outsiders were the ones to raise their voices the loudest against awful conditions.

Corporate greed is an easy target primarily because the historical record is consistent in telling the same tale: "big money" has been able to have its way because it has embedded itself with "big government"—this extends from policymakers to those who benefit financially from a happy business community. The only way exorbitant interest rates can be extracted from consumers via credit cards, mortgages and student loan payments is because the financial good of the banking industry is directly tied to national and state lawmakers. (It's good to remember that others who try to extract such payments are indicted on charges of extortion and racketeering.)

The same can be said of the medical-industrial complex of insurance and pharmaceutical companies. It's shameful enough that the medical establishment has kept several generations dependent on prescription drugs—how many kitchen counters and medicine cabinets, primarily those of the elderly, look like pharmacies? It's worse that, having created an epidemic of prescription-drug dependency, the same industrialists and government lackies make astronomical profits off of their victims. The defense of profiteering by pharmaceutical companies has been based in the cost of research; it's true enough that scientific research, so essential for the betterment of life, is very expensive, but where does all the research money go? If scientific research is funded by foundations, government grants and marathons, then the need to charge criminally high prices for lifesaving drugs comes only from greed.

There is much energy devoted to the issue of health-care "reform," but the reality is that there will be no reform until the system is brought under the control of real watchdogs. Reform will only happen when the profit margin is removed from the issue of health care. People are forced to seek health coverage in "the marketplace" and plagued by incessant advertisements from the medical and insurance industries. This marketplace is accepted and touted by both of the capitalistic ruling parties; we have made our physical and emotional well-being a commodity, and the public seems to have accepted it, again blindly trusting the shepherds who consistently fleece them.

When we view accessible health care like we view drinkable water and breathable air (with some scandalous exceptions—see Flint, Michigan), then we will have made a move toward real reform. One doesn't begrudge a homeless person or a person given the inhuman label of "illegal" of drinking water from a public fountain or breathing air that taxpaying citizens have helped to ensure. Why shouldn't health care be seen in the same light? If the argument against a broader view of health coverage is one of funding, then wouldn't it be more civilized if we pared down military spending, dispensing with the empire-building of an archaic mentality, to actually care for the real needs of all? Even if this is too much of a stretch, the yelling match in which this nation is engaged is even less grounded in the reality needed to find a solution. Socialists have demonstrated an ability to see things in a different light and have been successful, though often unrecognized, in pushing society further toward progress than the fearmongers who have held power for so long.

Chapter 10

BETWEEN A COBRA AND A PYTHON: WHERE DO WE GO FROM HERE?

Must we ever be under a system which makes every man a soldier—drains the country of her sons in the precious seed-time years…[a system] *which oppresses the treasury…makes mothers tremble when they look into the eyes of their first-born sons and think of these weary, weary, ever-recurring wars?*[125]
—*Editorial in* The Socialist, *1878*

Human history is most popularly learned as a record of wars raged on battlefields. The stories of weapons and strategies and personalities and acts of heroism (too often expressed in body counts) have defined the parameters of study. Over a period of time, guns rust, generals and government leaders die and borders and flags change; but people remain, sometimes in abject poverty and turned into refugees trampled underfoot by the armies marching through their streets, ignored by politicians culpable for dragging populations through the mud and blood of their ego-drenched decisions. But still, people survive. The pattern of history remains the same because leadership doesn't change—the drive for power, glory and wealth will probably always be present, but it can be tempered. That's what the role of government, of the rule of law, is meant to accomplish.

This is our template—that we are different from the rest of the animal kingdom and can use reason as the guide to tame the beasts inside of us. It's not the law of the jungle that reigns but the natural law that the ancients, almost three millennia ago, recognized as possible to reach—we can know "the Good," as Plato taught, and live according to our natural instincts to attain the good of all. If we cannot agree on a basic bottom line of what is good, then we're setting ourselves up for more of the same behavior—that the strong will overpower the weak and continue on the path to destruction that unchecked human behavior has spawned.

One of the few ways to reach this attainment is by opening our minds to what is possible but hasn't been tried. This work has sought to highlight the fragmented story of socialism in Chicago from its inception in 1876 as an organized political unit through its fights and near extinction after World War II. In the Atomic Age, the social upheavals from the 1960s onward have spurred people to seek alternatives to the game of political insiders playing by their own rules, "pay to play" cronyism and the restrictions on the number of players. Socialism has provided a way down a different path.

This book is a critique as much as it is a historical sketch. It proposes the possibility of a real alternative, not simply changing names on office doors—those doors must be widened and realigned. There are structural flaws in the building of the American republic, and they need to be adjusted periodically; this is the purpose of constitutional amendments. The Founding Fathers declared the right of the people to overthrow any government (like they did) when it strays from serving that same populace. The Constitution is written in a way that allows for less revolutionary change at any time with the support of the people. What is proposed in this little work is such a reappraisal—not with specifics, but with direction and precedent—that will recall the U.S. government to its original function: an entity created by the people, for the people, in order to serve the people.

Conditions around the world at this time demand a rethinking of the pattern of behavior of nations. This can only be achieved through serious self-reflection of individuals (an all-inclusive self-reflection, not an "us versus them" dichotomy). The stakes have been high for decades, with the extermination of life on Earth a real possibility since the splitting of the atom. Leaders of nations have jumped quickly into war, acted in accordance with the interests of the powerful and often neglected the multitudes who hold the true keys to power but too often have abdicated that power.

The people have often found themselves in a jungle, standing between a cobra and a python—the cobra strikes quickly and fatally; the python slowly squeezes its prey and then devours it, living on the corpse for days. This is the story of people throughout time and geography, microscopically studied through the Chicago experience. This is the exposure of a system that has attempted to strike down those who resist oppressive working conditions and inequitable living standards, and one that has slowly strangled an entire class of its own citizens and fed off of their labors. There is a path leading out of the jungle if only we can find the strength to follow it.

NOTES

Preface

1. George E. McNeill, *The Socialist*, "Letter to the Editor," June 21, 1879.

Chapter 1

2. Josephine Conger-Kaneko, "What a Socialist Alderman Would Do," the *Coming Nation*, March 1914.

Chapter 2

3. Taken from the English translation of the Egyptian fragment, "A Complaint from a Tomb Builder," in the Oriental Institute's Egyptian Museum at the University of Chicago (OIM 16991).
4. Jenz and Schneirov, *Chicago in the Age of Capital*, 24.
5. Ibid., 26.

Chapter 3

6. Illinois Legislative Special Committee on Labor, 3.

7. Parmet, *Labor and Immigration*, 20.

8. A culling of various issues of *The Socialist* from September 14 through November 9, 1878, brought forth the several policy planks of the party.

9. *Chicago Daily News*, April 3, 1877.

10. Hirsch, *Urban Revolt*, 30–35.

11. *The Socialist*, "Frank Stauber," March 29, 1879. (NB: all estimates in this book of cost adjustments over the years has been garnered from www.measuringworth.com using the Consumer Price Index average.)

12. *The Socialist*, "The Election," November 9, 1878.

13. *The Socialist*, "The Lesson," November 9, 1878.

14. Hirsch, *Urban Revolt*, 34–35.

15. http://www.encyclopedia.chicagohistory.org/chicagomayors, retrieved September 14, 2018.

16. *The Socialist*, "Fraud Did It," April 12, 1879.

17. *The Socialist*, "Intimidation of Voters," April 12, 1879.

18. Ibid.

19. Chicago Board of Election Commissioners, *Report, 1885–1915*, 9.

20. Ibid., 12–14.

21. Illinois Legislative Special Committee on Labor, *Report*, 3.

22. Ibid., 12–14.

23. Chicago Federation of Labor, *Labor and Pullman*, 5.

24. *Chicago Daily News*, "The Black Flag Unfurled," November 28, 1884.

25. *Daily Inter Ocean*, April 29, 1885.

26. This summary was retrieved from *Chicago Daily News* articles from June 30 through July 9, 1885.

27. *Chicago Daily News Almanac, 1885–1889*, August 26, 1886, 53–54 and September 1, 1886, 52.

Chapter 4

28. Bob Dylan, "The Times They Are A-Changin'," verse 3.

29. Hirsch, *Urban Revolt*, 24.

30. *The Socialist*, "A Crusade on Poverty," September 14, 1878.

31. Josephine Conger-Kaneko, the *Coming Nation*, "Placing the Blame," January 1914.

32. http://www.measuringworth.com, using the Consumer Price Index (CPI) estimates for 1878 and 2017, retrieved 9/30/18; *The Socialist*, "Benevolence," September 14, 1878.

33. City of Chicago Department of Development and Planning, *The People of Chicago*.

34. Behen, *The Chicago Labor Movement*, 11.

35. McCreesh, *On the Picket Line*, iii.

36. Chicago Federation of Labor, *Labor and Pullman*, 1–2.

37. Briggs and Peters, *Guide to the Pullman Company Archives*, vol. C in toto.

38. Ibid.

39. George F. Stone, ed., *Annual Report of Trade and Commerce of Chicago for 1900*, 44 and 19 (and George F. Stone, ed., *Annual Report of Trade and Commerce of Chicago for 1886*, 107).

40. Josephine Conger-Kaneko, the *Socialist Woman*, "Whited Sepulchers," February 1909.

41. U.S. Department of Labor, *History of Wages in the United States from Colonial Times to 1928*, 157–158, 165–166, 223–224, 229.

42. Chicago Bureau of Statistics, *City of Chicago Statistics, 1901–1902*, vol. I, nos. 1 and 2, xii.

43. Chicago Bureau of Statistics, *City of Chicago Statistics, 1905–1907*, vol. II, no. 4, appendix, ii.

44. Simons, *Class Struggle in America*, 12, 30.

45. Jenz and Schneirov, *Chicago in the Age of Capital*, 82.

46. John M. Work, the *Coming Nation*, "Is Socialism Right or Wrong," November 1913.

47. Simons, *Class Struggle in America*, 30.

48. Behen, *The Chicago Labor Movement*, 8.

49. Garb, *Freedom's Ballot*, 121.

50. Ibid., 119.

51. Ibid.

Chapter 5

52. *The Socialist*, "Who Are the Socialists?," September 14, 1878.

53. Parmet, *Labor and Immigration*, 46.

54. City of Chicago Department of Development and Planning, *The People of Chicago*.

55. Irving Cutler, *The Jews of Chicago: From Shtetl to Suburb* (Champaign: University of Illinois Press, 1996), 184.

56. Ibid., 185.

57. *Chicago Daily News*, gleaned from various issues, September 1–30, 1910.

58. Illinois General Assembly, *Working Conditions in Chicago in the Early 20ᵗʰ Century*, Vol. XXI, no. 2, November 1969, 151–152.

59. Ibid., 153–154.

60. First Black Workers Congress, September 5, 1971.

61. Garb, *Freedom's Ballot*, 139.

62. First Black Workers Congress, speech by John Watson, September 5, 1971.

63. "Lest We Forget: American Involvement in the First World War," Pritzker Military Museum and Library, retrieved on a visit on November 11, 2018.

64. Illinois State Council of Defense, *Report on Housing: Home Registration Service Commission, 1918*, 15.

65. Ibid., 11.

66. Ibid., 15–16.

67. William E. Walling, the *Socialist Woman*, "William E. Walling on Woman Suffrage," February 1909.

68. Josephine Conger-Kaneko, the *Socialist Woman*, "Victory Will Follow Knowledge," February 1909.

69. Ibid.

70. Josephine Conger-Kaneko, the *Socialist Woman*, "Chicago Socialist Women Held Suffrage Meeting," February 1909.

71. Josephine Conger-Kaneko, the *Socialist Woman*, "Intercollegiate Socialist Society," February 1909.

72. *Chicago Tribune*, "Illinois Women Oust 1,000 Bars," April 8, 1914.

73. Josephine Conger-Kaneko, the *Coming Nation*, "Results of the Woman Vote in Illinois," May–June 1914.

74. *Chicago Tribune*.

75. Conger-Kaneko.

76. *Chicago Tribune*.

77. Ibid., 8.

78. Josephine Conger-Kaneko, the *Coming Nation*, "Two Other Socialist Candidates for Alderman in Chicago," March 1914.

79. *Chicago Tribune*, February 4, 1914.

Chapter 6

80. Burke McCarty, the *Coming Nation*, "The Con Currency Bill," November 1913.

81. Josephine Conger-Kaneko, the *Progressive Woman*, "Dick Militia Bill," April 1909.
82. Josephine Conger-Kaneko, the *Coming Nation*, "Instead of Egg Strikes," December 1913.
83. Josephine Conger-Kaneko, the *Progressive Woman*, "The Things You Use Everyday," May 1909.
84. McCarty.
85. Leonard, ed., *The Book of Chicagoans*, 419.

Chapter 7

86. Uetricht, *Strike for America*, 3.
87. This information was gleaned from the various editions and volumes of the work of Ernest W. Burgess and Charles Newcome, *Census Data of the City of Chicago*.
88. Department of the Interior Census Office: Compendium of the Eleventh Census, 1890, Part 3, Population, 317 and 342.
89. Ibid.
90. Burgess and Newcome, 38.
91. Ibid., 33.
92. City of Chicago Bureau of Statistics, 1901–1902, vol. II, no. 1, Appendix.
93. Burgess and Newcome, 35.
94. "CPS Touts Increased Graduation Rate, Acknowledged Work Ahead," September 3, 2018, www.news.wttw.com.
95. Burgess and Newcome, 33, 52.
96. City of Chicago Planning and Development, Tax Increment Financing Program, retrieved November 19, 2018, www.cityofchicago.org.
97. Ben Joravsky, "Who Wins and Who Loses in Rahm's TIF Game?," retrieved November 29, 2018, www.chicagoreader.com.

Chapter 8

98. Aber, "Untitled Poem."
99. Advertisement in the *Coming Nation*, November 1913.
100. Advertisement in the *Coming Nation*, December 1913.
101. Advertisement in the *Coming Nation*, May–June 1914.
102. Advertisement in the *Socialist Woman*, March 1909.

103. cf. Barbara Tuchman, *The Guns of August*.

104. United States Postal Censor, "Letter from the U.S. Postal Censor to the Postmaster, R.J. Barry, Newberry Library, *Kerr Censorship Material*, Allen Ruff Papers, Series 2, Research Files, 1855–1997, Box G, Folder 188, nd.

105. William Haywood (1869–1928) was a founding member of the Industrial Workers of the World, along with Eugene Debs, Mary Marcy and others; United States Postal Censor.

106. Ibid.

107. Retrieved 12/6/18, www.clerk.house.gov; retrieved 12/6/18, www.senate.gov.

Chapter 9

108. Studs Terkel radio interview with Ralph Nader, June 23, 1968.

109. www.encyclopedia.chicagohistory.org/chicagomayors.

110. *Chicago Tribune*, "Daley Sweeps to Sixth Term," April 2, 1975.

111. Ibid.

112. *Chicago Tribune*, "Daley Praises Police," April 1, 1975.

113. Socialist Party of Illinois, *Bulletin No. 4*.

114. First Black Workers Congress, John Watson speech, September 5, 1971.

115. Ibid.

116. Harold Brown, ed., Michele Russell, First Black Workers Congress, September 5, 1971.

117. Welfare Council of Metro Chicago, "1970 Census Data," General Population and Housing Characteristics, Report No. Three, 1.

118. Wurman, *Understanding USA*.

119. Wurman, *Understanding USA*.

120. "Chicago Democracy Project," accessed September 13, 2018, www.chicagodemocracy.org.

121. www.census.gov., accessed 12/17/18.

122. Press release, Socialist Party of Illinois.

123. Studs Terkel radio interview with Ralph Nader, June 23, 1968.

124. Ibid.

Chapter 10

125. *The Socialist*, "The Spirit of Unrest," September 14, 1878.

BIBLIOGRAPHY

ANNOTATED BIBLIOGRAPHY OF SOURCES CITED

Aber, Loureine. "Untitled Poem." Dill Pickle Club Records, 1906–1941, Box 3, Folder 290, Writings and Poems: A–L. Housed at the Newberry Library.

    The poem is filed with much material from Chicago's eclectic Dill Pickle Club, which met just steps away from the group's archival home at the Newberry Library. The collection gives a clear and personal picture of this group of local and national celebrities and their written work. I even stumbled across a poem about my hometown: "South Bend, Indiana: Impressions."

Behen, David M. *The Chicago Labor Movement, 1874–1896.* Doctoral diss., University of Chicago, August 1953.

    A solid work that helps to put the labor events of the late nineteenth century in clearer perspective, particularly the "Great Upheaval" of 1877, the Haymarket Riot of 1886 and the Pullman Strike of 1894.

Briggs, Martha T., and Cynthia H. Peters. *Guide to the Pullman Company Archives.* Chicago: Newberry Library, 1995.

    This work is a monumental task accomplished at the end of the last century to the benefit of researchers looking into the history of the Pullman Company and its management, workers and the infamous strike. I only delved into one particular piece located under the following thread: Record

Group No. 6, Employee and Labor Relations, Subgroup No. 2, Personnel Administration, Series 06, Discharge and Release Records, 1880–1957, Vol. C, 1890–1895.

Burgess, Ernest W., and Charles Newcomb. *Census Data of the City of Chicago, 1920.* Chicago: University of Chicago Press, 1931.
   This compilation is an invaluable resource from which I gleaned much information regarding work, education, race and age in Chicago in the decade after the First World War.

Chicago Board of Election Commissioners. *Report, 1885–1915.* Chicago: 1915.
   This resource chronicles, quite honestly, the rampant corruption of the city's electoral machine before the first steps toward reform were taken after the notoriously crooked 1883 municipal elections. In a sense, it's a "Thirtieth Jubilee" commemoration that can serve to recall the people of today, over 130 years removed from the events chronicled in this report, to greater vigilance regarding the sanctity of the vote.

Chicago Federation of Labor. *Labor and Pullman, 1884–1994: Pullman Porter Strike Scrapbook, May 6–August 31, 1894.* Chicago: Chicago Federation of Labor, 1994.
   This folio archive gives a solid chronology for the causes, events and end of the first major labor dispute to occur in Chicago since the Haymarket Riot.

Chicago History Museum, microfilm collection, including the *Chicago Daily News*, *Chicago Daily Tribune*, *Chicago Tribune*, *Daily Inter Ocean* and *The Socialist*. Dates of the periodicals in the collection range from 1877 to 1975.
   The microfilm collection of the museum was a treasure trove of information on specific topics related to my research as well as side stories of particular times. A single visit to the research center and an hour or two at the microfilm projector will yield an experience as close to time travel as one can get outside of the world of fiction.

City of Chicago Bureau of Statistics. *Statistics.* Chicago: Chicago Municipal Library and Bureau of Statistics, 1901–1907.
   This compilation provides a vast amount of information on education and labor in Chicago at the beginning of the twentieth century.

City of Chicago Department of Development and Planning. *The People of Chicago: Who We Are and Who We Have Been*. Chicago: Department of Development and Planning, 1976.

    This is another vital resource filled with various statistics that allowed me to follow the life of the people of Chicago into the contemporary time.

Conger-Kaneko, Josephine. The *Socialist Woman* (1907–1909), the *Progressive Woman* (1909–1913) and the *Coming Nation* (1913–1914). Chicago: The Socialist Woman Publishing Co. Housed at the Newberry Library.

    Conger-Kaneko, while one of many unmentioned in most history books, was one of the leading journalists/editors of her time in Chicago. While trumpeting a particular left-leaning perspective, the articles in all of the issues of these three periodicals give voice to oft-ignored positions on politics, economics, religion, race, ethnicity, labor and education, in addition to women's issues.

Encyclopedia of Chicago. University of Chicago Press: Chicago, 2004.

    This epic informational work is an essential resource for anyone wishing to gain any foundational knowledge of the city. The hardback edition is a handsome addition to a researcher's bookcase, and the online edition, found at www.encyclopedia.chicago.history.org, is readily available to carry around while one is on the go.

First Black Workers Congress. Speeches and Papers. Gary, Indiana: September 5, 1971.

    This is one of the first organizations in the post–World War II era to address the issue of African American and Latin American workers from a more Marxist approach to history and economics.

Garb, Margaret. *Freedom's Ballot: African-American Political Struggles*. Chicago: University of Chicago Press, 2014.

    This is a unique account of the roots of the ongoing fight for equality of voice in African American communities since the Emancipation Proclamation and related constitutional amendments of the Reconstruction era.

Hirsch, Eric L. *Urban Revolt*. Berkeley: University of California Press, 1990.

    Hirsch's work is a solid resource for the biggest chance Socialists had in the nineteenth century to overturn the political machine in Chicago—the municipal elections of 1877 and 1879.

Illinois Bureau of Labor Statistics. *Bureau of the Census, 1880–81, 1884, 1888–1908*. Washington, D.C.: U.S. Government Printing Office, 1910.
   Statistics are a tricky item to include in any work, as they can be easily manipulated. I have tried to show, in a very limited way, some patterns (wages, age ranges, occupations) that can be harvested from the census records.

Illinois General Assembly. *Working Conditions in Chicago in the Early Twentieth Century*. American Jewish Archives, November 1969.
   This is a good resource for the state's reports on the conditions of the laboring masses prior to the First World War as chronicled in the American Jewish Archives.

Illinois Legislative Special Committee on Labor. *Report*. Springfield: Weber, Magie and Company, 1879.
   This is a solid resource for research in that the state's good intentions are recorded, as are the names of the lesser-known legislators and labor leaders in Chicago in the 1870s.

Illinois State Council of Defense. *Home Registration Service Committee's Report on Housing*. 1918.
   This report serves as a record of the state's effort to alleviate problems of transportation for the workers on Chicago's south side and in Indiana's northwest corner.

Jenz, John B., and Richard Schneirov. *Chicago in the Age of Capital: Class, Politics and Democracy*. Urbana: University of Illinois Press, 2012.
   This is a pivotal work in contemporary research on the issues related to Chicago's labor history in the latter half of the nineteenth century and into the twentieth.

Kerr Censorship Material. *Allen Ruff Papers*, Series 2: Research Files, 1855–1997, Box 6, Folder 188. Housed at the Newberry Library.
   This is a vast amount of material, even though I only focused on censorship material from 1917 to 1919. Government documents, personal correspondence and other evidence of covert and overt persecution of left-leaning people in the Chicago area would provide enough material for a book on this period alone—but, alas, perhaps for another day.

Leonard, John W., ed., *The Book of Chicagoans: A Biographical Dictionary of Leading Living Men of the City of Chicago*. Chicago: A.N. Marquis, 1905.

This is a unique resource of names and occupations of Chicago's leaders (in later editions, expanded to include women) as well as the lesser-known personalities in the city.

McCreesh, Carolyn D. *On the Picket Line: Militant Women, 1880–1917*. Doctoral diss., University of Maryland, 1975.

This work gives a good background to some of the pivotal personalities related to women in the workplace in the pre–Nineteenth Amendment era. It is a solid work for discovering the names of lesser-known women in the garment industry of Chicago at the time of the strikes of 1910–15.

Parmet, Robert D. *Labor and Immigration in Industrial America*. Boston: G.K. Hall, 1981.

Parmet's work offers a basic understanding of the relationship between workers of all backgrounds and the industries in which they labored at the beginning of the post–Civil War era.

Simons, Algie Martin. *Class Struggle in America*. Chicago: Charles Kerr, 1903.

Simons, one of the leading philosophical socialists of his day, presents a work that is a strongly-worded indictment of industrialization, mechanization at the expense of the wage worker and imperialism as was witnessed after the Spanish-American War.

Socialist Party of Illinois. *Bulletin No. 4: John Quinn Brisben Mayoral Write-In Candidacy*. March 18, 1975.

A surviving testimony to a truly grassroots effort, this bulletin was a mimeographed copy calling on last-minute support for a man who was prohibited from placing himself on the ballot in Chicago due to the disparate number of necessary signatures required of candidates from minor political parties as compared to those from the major parties.

The Socialist, September 14, 1878–August 16, 1879. Chicago History Museum, microfilm collection. ("Miscellaneous Chicago Newspapers, 1843–1917.")

This late-nineteenth and early-twentieth-century newspaper was a valuable resource for contemporary accounts of events from an alternative (not mainstream) source in Chicago. Though the quality of microfilm limited readability at times, and the issues that have survived intact are limited, reading through the extant texts is a gift to be appreciated by anyone looking for long-suppressed voices of change.

Uetricht, Micah. *Strike for America: Chicago Teachers Against Austerity*. Chicago: Verso, 2014.
Uetricht's work chronicles the 2012 Chicago Teachers Strike, its causes, the rationale behind its success and the ongoing challenges of education in the city and around the country. This is a handy piece to keep around to build up intellectual arguments for change in many areas of the city and nation.

Welfare Council of Metro Chicago. *1970 Census Data: General Population and Housing Characteristics*, reports 1, 2, and 3. Chicago: Welfare Council of Metro Chicago, 1971.
As part of the federal program of the late 1960s called Model Cities, of which Chicago was named a "Model City Target Area," the Welfare Council's report studied housing issues in the city with the goal of improving the living conditions in many blighted areas.

Wurman, Richard Saul, ed. *Understanding USA*. Newport, RI: TED Conferences, 1999.
These TED Talks, compiled in one work, give a graphic understanding of the status of Chicago and the nation regarding wealth and employment.

ANNOTATED BIBLIOGRAPHY OF RESOURCES FOR FURTHER STUDY

Abbot, Edith. *The Wages of Unskilled Labor in the U.S., 1850–1900*. Chicago: University of Chicago Press, 1905. This is a helpful resource for a clear picture of different occupations and wages in the last half of the nineteenth century.

Carsel, Wilfred. *A History of the Chicago Ladies' Garment Workers' Union*. Chicago: Normandie House, 1940. Carsel's work is the most complete chronicle of the events leading up to the formation of this union and the garment workers' strikes of 1910, 1914 and 1915.

Conger-Kaneko, Josephine. *The Labor Martyrs Project.* "Hellraisers Journal." www.weneverforget.org. This is a digitized archive of more of Conger-Kaneko's work and further information about her.

Cowell, Frank Richard. *Cicero and the Roman Republic.* Baltimore: Pelican Books, 1964. This is a classic work of late Republican Roman history and a solid resource for the life of everyday citizens in antiquity.

Cullum, Shelby M. *Fifty Years of Public Service.* Chicago: A.C. McClurg, 1911. This is a somewhat touching autobiography of the Illinois representative, U.S. representative, U.S. senator and Illinois governor who lived from 1829 until 1914.

Heideman, Paul. "Socialism and Black Oppression." *Jacobin*, April 30, 2018. https://jacobinmag.com/2018/04/socialism-marx-race-class-struggle-color-line. The website is solidly left-leaning, and the article cited outlines the main socialist position that racial oppression, as it has played out in this hemisphere, is primarily an economic issue, with race used as the primary vehicle of oppression.

International Socialist Review. www.isreview.org. The online contemporary journal promotes the theories and philosophies of the Socialist Party in the nation and around the world. The original ISR was printed in Chicago from 1900 to 1918 and is accessible online as well.

Materson, Lisa. *For the Freedom of Her Race: Black Women and Electoral Politics, 1877–1932.* Chapel Hill: University of North Carolina Press, 2009. This is a pivotal work in the area of post–Reconstruction era African American history as well as the issue of women's suffrage before, during and after the Nineteenth Amendment was passed. Sadly, the political focus remained in relation to the Democratic and Republican Parties only.

Orwell, George. "The Lion and the Unicorn: Socialism and the English Genius." In *Why I Write.* New York: Penguin, 2005. This essay is essential reading for anyone wishing to gain an understanding of a workable socialism in the United States. Orwell makes a clear distinction between Stalinism and the economic structure he was advocating for during the Second World War.

Roediger, David R. *The Wages of Whiteness: Race and the Making of the American Working Class*. London: Verso, 1991. Roediger's book is a good introduction into the roots of strife among workers in the United States and how racial differences have been used to widen the gap between white and black workers in the Industrial Age.

Rousseau, Jean-Jacques. *A Discourse on Inequality*. New York: Penguin Books, 1984. This is a foundational piece of Enlightenment philosophy and a good introduction to understanding social and economic differences in people.

Stone, George F. *Chicago Board of Trade 29th Annual Report of the Trade and Commerce of Chicago, for the Year Ending December 31, 1886*. Chicago: Knight and Leonard, 1887. This is one of many reports that made researching data much easier. The information was plentiful (and mostly unnecessary for this book) and provided a fascinating detour into the wealth accumulated in the city over the period of various years.

Storrs, Emery A. *The Dedication of the New Board of Trade Building, Chicago, April 29, 1885*. Chicago: R.R. Donnelley and Sons, 1915. The program of the dedication evening is preserved in this archival collection. It's an interesting piece in that it shows the event from the perspective of the guests and dignitaries, not of those participating in the protest rally and march that was happening outside.

U.S. Department of Commerce. Bureau of the Census. *Census Abstracts, 12th Census of the U.S., 1880: Manufacturers*. Vol. 2. Washington, D.C.: U.S. Government Printing Office, 1881.

———. Bureau of the Census. *Census Abstracts, 16th Census of the U.S., 1940: Population and Housing*. Washington, D.C.: U.S. Government Printing Office, 1943.

———. Bureau of Labor. *10th Annual Report of the Commissioner of Labor, 1894, Strikes and Lockouts*.

U.S. Department of Commerce and Labor. Bureau of the Census. *A Century of Population Growth: 1790–1900*. Washington, D.C.: U.S. Government Printing Office, 1909.

U.S. Department of Labor. *History of Wages in the United States from Colonial Times to 1928*. Washington, D.C.: U.S. Government Printing Office, 1929.

U.S. Department of the Interior. Census Office. *Compendium of the Eleventh Census, 1890*. Washington, D.C.: U.S. Government Printing Office, 1898.

U.S. House of Representatives. *Investigation by a Select Committee of the House of Representatives Relative to the Causes of the General Depression in Labor and Business; and as to Chinese Immigration*. 46th Congress, 2nd Session. Washington, D.C.: U.S. Government Printing Office. 1879.

U.S. Senate. *Report of Women and Child Wage Earners in the U.S.* Senate Doc. 645, 61st Congress, 2nd Session, 1910. Vols. 2 and 9.

www.weneverforget.org. "The Labor Martyrs Project" is a contemporary website dedicated to the promotion of people and events relevant to the labor movement in the United States. It's well-documented and up to date, with regular weekly posts of articles, past and present, as well as photographs to present a valuable chronicle of a significant piece of American history.

INDEX

V

Vasquez, Andre 51

W

Walling, William E. 71
Warren, James 99
Watson, John 97
Williams, Eugene 69
Work, John M. 59
Wright, Carroll D. 65

Y

Yerkes, Charles 60

Z

Zebh, Nellie 73

ABOUT THE AUTHOR

Courtesy of Nathanael Filbert.

Joseph Anthony Rulli is a transplanted Hoosier who has been living in Chicago since the fall of 2006. He has taught social studies, religion, philosophy and history at a high school level in Indiana. He began writing as a career upon his arrival to his second city and has had three short stories published, "The Meating" (*New Stone Circle*, 2009), "Delayed" (*Echo Ink Review*, 2009) and "With This Ring" (*Over the Edge: The Edgy Writers Anthology*, 2017); a stage play (*Let Me Just Say This*) performed in 2016; an electronic tour book (*The Working Class Smells…So Do Roses*) published online in 2014; and is the author of *The Chicago Haymarket Affair* (The History Press, 2016). He has written a regular column and cultural reviews for the *Chicago Grid* and *Picture This Post*. This work is his second book for The History Press.

Visit us at
www.historypress.com